# Heralds of God's Word

## Lay Preaching Seminar
## Workbook

by Mike Stickland
edited by Joel Sarli

General Conference Ministerial Association

Copyright © 1998
Ministerial Association
General Conference of Seventh-day Adventists

PRINTED IN U.S.A.
Pacific Press Publishing Association
Nampa, ID 83687


ISBN 1-57847-053-6

# Workbook Contents

# Assignments: Lesson 1

## Every Believer a Preacher

**Class assignment:**
Attend the tutorial "Every Believer a Preacher" and read the related class notes.

**Reading assignment:**
E. G. White: *The Desire of Ages,* Chapter 8, "The Passover Visit."

**Written assignment:**
What do you think are the main factors in growing a strong Christian experience from which you may develop a lay-preacher ministry? Write a brief explanation.

**Reading**
Ellen G. White, *The Desire of Ages* 75-83.

"The Passover Visit"

Among the Jews the twelfth year was the dividing line between childhood and youth. On completing this year a Hebrew boy was called a son of the law, and also a son of God. He was given special opportunities for religious instruction, and was expected to participate in the sacred feasts and observances. It was in accordance with this custom that Jesus in His boyhood made the Passover visit to Jerusalem. Like all devout Israelites, Joseph and Mary went up every year to attend the Passover; and when Jesus had reached the required age, they took Him with them.

There were three annual feasts, the Passover, the Pentecost, and the Feast of Tabernacles, at which all the men of Israel were commanded to appear before the Lord at Jerusalem. Of these feasts the Passover was the most largely attended. Many were present from all countries where the Jews were scattered. From every part of Palestine the worshipers came in great numbers. The journey from Galilee occupied several days, and the travelers united in large companies for companionship and protection.

The women and aged men rode upon oxen or asses over the steep and rocky roads. The stronger men and the youth journeyed on foot. The time of the Passover corresponded to the close of March or the beginning of April, and the whole land was bright with flowers, and glad with the song of birds. All along the way were spots memorable in the history of Israel, and fathers and mothers recounted to their children the wonders that God had wrought for His people in ages past. They beguiled their journey with song and music, and when at last the towers of Jerusalem came into view, every voice joined in the triumphant strain,—

"Our feet shall stand
Within thy gates, O Jerusalem. . . .
Peace be within thy walls,
And prosperity within thy palaces."
    Ps. 122:2-7.

The observance of the Passover began with the birth of the Hebrew nation. On the last night of their bondage in Egypt, when there appeared no token of deliverance, God commanded them to prepare for an immediate release. He had warned Pharaoh of the final judgment on the Egyptians, and He directed the Hebrews to gather their families within their own dwellings. Having sprinkled the doorposts with the blood of the slain lamb, they were to eat the lamb, roasted, with unleavened bread and bitter herbs. "And thus shall ye eat it," He said, "with your loins girded, your shoes on your feet, and your staff in your hand; and ye shall eat it in haste: it is the Lord's Passover." Ex. 12:11. At midnight all the first-born of the Egyptians were slain. Then the king sent to Israel the message, "Rise up, and get you forth from among my people; . . . and go, serve the Lord, as ye have said." Ex. 12:31. The Hebrews went out from Egypt an independent nation. The Lord had commanded that the Passover should be yearly kept. "It shall come to pass," He said, "when your children shall say unto you, What mean ye by this service? that ye shall say, It is the sacrifice of the Lord's Passover, who passed over the houses of the children of Israel in Egypt, when He smote the Egyptians." Thus from generation to generation the story of this wonderful deliverance was to be repeated.

The Passover was followed by the seven days' feast of unleavened bread. On the second day of the feast, the first fruits of the year's harvest, a sheaf of barley, was presented before the Lord. All the ceremonies of the feast were types of the work of Christ. The deliverance of Israel from Egypt was an object lesson of redemption, which the Passover was intended to keep in memory. The slain lamb, the unleavened bread, the sheaf of first fruits, represented the Saviour.

With most of the people in the days of Christ, the observance of this feast had degenerated into formalism. But what was its significance to the Son of God!

For the first time the child Jesus looked upon the temple. He saw the white-robed priests performing their solemn ministry. He beheld the bleeding victim upon the altar of sacrifice. With the worshipers He bowed in prayer, while the cloud of incense ascended before God. He witnessed the impressive rites of the paschal service. Day by day He saw their meaning more clearly. Every act seemed to be bound up with His own life. New impulses were awakening within Him. Silent and absorbed, He seemed to be studying out a great problem. The mystery of His mission was opening to the Saviour.

Rapt in the contemplation of these scenes, He did not remain beside His parents. He sought to be alone. When the paschal services were ended, He still lingered in the temple courts; and when the worshipers departed from Jerusalem, He was left behind.

In this visit to Jerusalem, the parents of Jesus wished to bring Him in connection with the great teachers in Israel. While He was obedient in every particular to the word of God, He did not conform to the rabbinical rites and usages. Joseph and Mary hoped that He might be led to reverence the learned rabbis, and give more diligent heed to their requirements. But Jesus in the temple had been taught by God. That which He had received, He began at once to impart.

At that day an apartment connected with the temple was devoted to a sacred school, after the manner of the schools of the prophets. Here leading rabbis with their pupils assembled, and hither the child Jesus came. Seating Himself at the feet of these grave, learned men, He listened to their instruction. As one seeking for wisdom, He questioned these teachers in regard to the prophecies, and to events then taking place that pointed to the advent of the Messiah.

Jesus presented Himself as one thirsting for a knowledge of God. His questions were suggestive of deep truths which had long been obscured, yet which were vital to the salvation of souls. While showing how narrow and superficial was the wisdom of the wise men, every question put before them a divine lesson, and placed truth in a new aspect. The rabbis spoke of the wonderful elevation which the Messiah's coming would bring to the Jewish nation; but Jesus presented the prophecy of Isaiah, and asked them the meaning of those scriptures that point to the suffering and death of the Lamb of God.

The doctors turned upon Him with questions, and they were amazed at His answers. With the humility of a child He repeated the words of Scripture, giving them a depth of meaning that the wise men had not conceived of. If followed, the lines of truth He pointed out would have worked a reformation in the religion of the day. A deep interest in spiritual things would have been awakened; and when Jesus began His ministry, many would have been prepared to receive Him.

The rabbis knew that Jesus had not been instructed in their schools; yet His understanding of the prophecies far exceeded theirs. In this thoughtful Galilean boy they discerned great promise. They desired to gain Him as a student, that He might become a teacher in Israel. They wanted to have charge of His education, feeling that a mind so original must be brought under their molding.

The words of Jesus had moved their hearts as they had never before been moved by words from human lips. God was seeking to give light to those leaders in Israel, and He used the only means by which they could be reached. In their pride they would have scorned to admit that they could receive instruction from anyone. If Jesus had appeared to be trying to teach them, they would have disdained to listen. But they flattered themselves that they were teaching Him, or at least testing His knowledge of the Scriptures. The youthful modesty and grace of Jesus disarmed their prejudices. Unconsciously their minds were opened to the word of God, and the Holy Spirit spoke to their hearts.

They could not but see that their expectation in regard to the Messiah was not sustained by prophecy; but they would not renounce the theories that had flattered their ambition. They would not admit that they had misapprehended the Scriptures they claimed to teach. From one to another passed the inquiry, How hath this youth knowledge, having never learned? The light was shining in darkness; but "the darkness apprehended it not." John 1:5, R. V.

Meanwhile Joseph and Mary were in great perplexity and distress. In the departure from Jerusalem they had lost sight of Jesus, and they knew not that He had tarried behind. The country was then densely populated, and the caravans from Galilee were very large. There was much confusion as they left the city. On the way the pleasure of traveling with friends and acquaintances absorbed their attention, and they did not notice His absence till night came on. Then as they halted for rest, they missed the helpful hand of their child. Supposing Him to be with their company, they had felt no anxiety. Young as He was, they had trusted Him implicitly, expecting that when needed, He would be ready to assist them, anticipating their wants as He had always done. But now their fears were roused. They searched for Him throughout their company, but in vain. Shuddering they remembered how Herod had tried to destroy Him in His infancy. Dark forebodings filled their hearts. They bitterly reproached themselves.

Returning to Jerusalem, they pursued their search. The next day, as they mingled with the worshipers in the temple, a familiar voice arrested their attention. They could not mistake it; no other voice was like His, so serious and earnest, yet so full of melody.

In the school of the rabbis they found Jesus. Rejoiced as they were, they could not forget their grief and anxiety. When He was with them again, the mother said, in words that implied reproof, "Son, why hast Thou thus dealt with us? Behold, Thy father and I have sought Thee sorrowing."

"How is it that ye sought Me?" answered Jesus. "Wist ye not that I must be about My Father's business?" And as they seemed not to understand His words, He pointed upward. On His face was a light at which they wondered. Divinity was flashing through humanity. On finding Him in the temple, they had listened to what was passing between Him and the rabbis, and they were astonished at His questions and answers. His words started a train of thought that would never be forgotten.

And His question to them had a lesson. "Wist ye not," He said, "that I must be about My Father's business?" Jesus was engaged in the work that He had come into the world to do; but Joseph and Mary had neglected theirs. God had shown them high honor in committing to them His Son. Holy angels had directed the course of Joseph in order to preserve the life of Jesus. But for an entire day they had lost sight of Him whom they should not have forgotten for a moment. And when their anxiety was relieved, they had not censured themselves, but had cast the blame upon Him.

It was natural for the parents of Jesus to look upon Him as their own child. He was daily with them, His life in many respects was like that of other children, and it was difficult for them to realize that He was the Son of God. They were in danger of failing to appreciate the blessing granted them in the presence of the world's Redeemer. The grief of their separation from Him, and the gentle reproof which His words conveyed, were designed to impress them with the sacredness of their trust.

In the answer to His mother, Jesus showed for the first time that He understood His relation to God. Before His birth the angel had said to Mary, "He shall be great, and shall be called the Son of the Highest: and the Lord God shall give unto Him the throne of His father David: and He shall reign over the house of Jacob forever." Luke 1:32, 33. These words Mary had pondered in her heart; yet while she believed that her child was to be Israel's Messiah, she did not comprehend His mission. Now she did not understand His words; but she knew that He had disclaimed kinship to Joseph, and had declared His Sonship to God.

Jesus did not ignore His relation to His earthly parents. From Jerusalem He returned home with them, and aided them in their life of toil. He hid in His own heart the mystery of His mission, waiting submissively for the appointed time for Him to enter upon His work. For eighteen years after He had recognized that He was the Son of God, He acknowledged the tie that bound Him to the home at Nazareth, and performed the duties of a son, a brother, a friend, and a citizen.

As His mission had opened to Jesus in the temple, He shrank from contact with the multitude. He wished to return from Jerusalem in quietness, with those who knew the secret of His life. By the paschal service, God was seeking to call His people away from their worldly cares, and to remind them of His wonderful work in their deliverance from Egypt. In this work He desired them to see a promise of deliverance from sin. As the blood of the slain lamb sheltered the homes of Israel, so the blood of Christ was to save their souls; but they could be saved through Christ only as by faith they should make His life their own. There was virtue in the symbolic service only as it directed the worshipers to Christ as their personal Saviour. God desired that they should be led to prayerful study and meditation in regard to Christ's mission. But as the multitudes left Jerusalem, the excitement of travel and social intercourse too often absorbed their attention, and the service they had witnessed was forgotten. The Saviour was not attracted to their company.

As Joseph and Mary should return from Jerusalem alone with Jesus, He hoped to direct their minds to the prophecies of the suffering Saviour. Upon Calvary He sought to lighten His mother's grief. He was thinking of her now. Mary was to witness His last agony, and Jesus desired her to understand His mission, that she might be strengthened to endure, when the sword should pierce through her soul. As Jesus had been separated from her, and she had sought Him sorrowing three days, so when He should be offered up for the sins of the world, He would again be lost to her for three days. And as He should come forth from the tomb, her sorrow would again be turned to joy. But how much better she could have borne the anguish of His death if she had understood the Scriptures to which He was now trying to turn her thoughts!

If Joseph and Mary had stayed their minds upon God by meditation and prayer, they would have realized the sacredness of their trust, and would not have lost sight of Jesus. By one day's neglect they lost the Saviour; but it cost them three days of anxious search to find Him. So with us; by idle talk, evilspeaking, or neglect of prayer, we may in one day lose the Saviour's presence, and it may take many days of sorrowful search to find Him, and regain the peace that we have lost.

In our association with one another, we should take heed lest we forget Jesus, and pass along unmindful that He is not with us. When we become absorbed in worldly things so that we have no thought for Him in whom our hope of eternal life is centered, we separate ourselves from Jesus and from the heavenly angels. These holy beings cannot remain where the Saviour's presence is not desired, and His absence is not marked. This is why discouragement so often exists among the professed followers of Christ.

Many attend religious services, and are refreshed and comforted by the word of God; but through neglect of meditation, watchfulness, and prayer, they lose the blessing, and find themselves more destitute than before they received it. Often they feel that God has dealt hardly with them. They do not see that the fault is their own. By separating themselves from Jesus, they have shut away the light of His presence.

It would be well for us to spend a thoughtful hour each day in contemplation of the life of Christ. We should take it point by point, and let the imagination grasp each scene, especially the closing ones. As we thus dwell upon His great sacrifice for us, our confidence in Him will be more constant, our love will be quickened, and we shall be more deeply imbued with His spirit. If we would be saved at last, we must learn the lesson of penitence and humiliation at the foot of the cross.

As we associate together, we may be a blessing to one another. If we are Christ's, our sweetest thoughts will be of Him. We shall love to talk of Him; and as we speak to one another of His love, our hearts will be softened by divine influences. Beholding the beauty of His character, we shall be "changed into the same image from glory to glory." 2 Cor. 3:18.

# Assignments: Lesson 2

## It's Like Growing a Garden

**Class assignment:**

Attend the tutorial "It's Like Growing a Garden" and read the related class notes.

**Reading assignment:**

E. G. White, *The Acts of the Apostles*, Chapter 2, "The Training of the Twelve."

**Written assignment:**

Based on your reading of the assignment from *The Acts of the Apostles*, write a brief summary of what you believe is the most important preparation you will make to become a (better) lay preacher.

**Reading**

Ellen G. White, *The Acts of the Apostles* 17-24.

"The Training of the Twelve"

For the carrying on of His work, Christ did not choose the learning or eloquence of the Jewish Sanhedrin or the power of Rome. Passing by the self-righteous Jewish teachers, the Master Worker chose humble, unlearned men to proclaim the truths that were to move the world. These men He purposed to train and educate as the leaders of His church. They in turn were to educate others and send them out with the gospel message. That they might have success in their work they were to be given the power of the Holy Spirit. Not by human might or human wisdom was the gospel to be proclaimed, but by the power of God.

For three years and a half the disciples were under the instruction of the greatest Teacher the world has ever known. By personal contact and association, Christ trained them for His service. Day by day they walked and talked with Him, hearing His words of cheer to the weary and heavy-laden, and seeing the manifestation of His power in behalf of the sick and the afflicted. Sometimes He taught them, sitting among them on the mountainside; sometimes beside the sea or walking by the way, He revealed the mysteries of the kingdom of God. Wherever hearts were open to receive the divine message, He unfolded the truths of the way of salvation. He did not command the disciples to do this or that, but said, "Follow Me." On His journeys through country and cities, He took them with Him, that they might see how He taught the people. They traveled with Him from place to place. They shared His frugal fare, and like Him were sometimes hungry and often weary. On the crowded streets, by the lakeside, in the lonely desert, they were with Him. They saw Him in every phase of life.

It was at the ordination of the Twelve that the first step was taken in the organization of the church that after Christ's departure was to carry on His work on the earth. Of this ordination the record says, "He goeth up into a mountain, and calleth unto Him whom He would: and they came unto Him. And He ordained twelve, that they should be with Him, and that He might send them forth to preach." Mark 3:13, 14.

Look upon the touching scene. Behold the Majesty of heaven surrounded by the Twelve whom He has chosen. He is about to set them apart for their work. By these feeble agencies, through His word and Spirit, He designs to place salvation within the reach of all.

With gladness and rejoicing, God and the angels beheld this scene. The Father knew that from these men the light of heaven would shine forth; that the words spoken by them as they witnessed for His Son, would echo from generation to generation till the close of time.

The disciples were to go forth as Christ's witnesses, to declare to the world what they had seen and heard of Him. Their office was the most important to which human beings had ever been called, second only to that of Christ Himself. They were to be workers together with God for the saving of men. As in the Old Testament the twelve patriarchs stood as representatives of Israel, so the twelve apostles stand as representatives of the gospel church.

During His earthly ministry Christ began to break down the partition wall between Jew and Gentile, and to preach salvation to all mankind. Though He was a Jew, He mingled freely with the Samaritans, setting at nought the Pharisaic customs of the Jews with regard to this despised people. He slept under their roofs, ate at their tables, and taught in their streets.

The Saviour longed to unfold to His disciples the truth regarding the breaking down of the "middle wall of partition" between Israel and the other nations—the truth that "the Gentiles should be fellow heirs" with the Jews and "partakers of His promise in Christ by the gospel." Ephesians 2:14; 3:6. This truth was revealed in part at the time when He rewarded the faith of the centurion at Capernaum, and also when He preached the gospel to the inhabitants of Sychar. Still more plainly was it revealed on the occasion of His visit to Phoenicia, when He healed the daughter of the Canaanite woman. These experiences helped the disciples to understand that among those whom many regarded as unworthy of salvation, there were souls hungering for the light of truth.

Thus Christ sought to teach the disciples the truth that in God's kingdom there are no territorial lines, no caste, no aristocracy; that they must go to all nations, bearing to them the message of a Saviour's love. But not until later did they realize in all its fullness that God "hath made of one blood all nations of men for to dwell on all the face of the earth, and hath determined the times before appointed, and the bounds of their habitation; that they should seek the Lord, if haply they might feel after Him, and find Him, though He be not far from every one of us." Acts 17:26, 27.

In these first disciples was presented marked diversity. They were to be the world's teachers, and they represented widely varied types of character. In order successfully to carry forward the work to which they had been called, these men, differing in natural characteristics and in habits of life, needed to come into unity of feeling, thought, and action. This unity it was Christ's object to secure. To this end He sought to bring them into unity with Himself. The burden of His labor for them is expressed in His prayer to His Father, "That they all may be one; as Thou, Father, art in Me, and I in Thee, that they also may be one in Us;" "that the world may know that Thou has sent Me, and hast loved them, as Thou hast loved Me." John 17:21, 23. His constant prayer for them was that they might be sanctified through the truth; and He prayed with assurance, knowing that an Almighty decree had been given before the world was made. He knew that the gospel of the kingdom would be preached to all nations for a witness; He knew that truth armed with the omnipotence of the Holy Spirit, would conquer in the battle with evil, and that the bloodstained banner would one day wave triumphantly over His followers.

As Christ's earthly ministry drew to a close, and He realized that He must soon leave His disciples to carry on the work without His personal supervision, He sought to encourage them and to prepare them for the future. He did not deceive them with false hopes. As an open book He read what was to be. He knew He was about to be separated from them, to leave them as sheep among wolves. He knew that they would suffer persecution, that they would be cast out of the synagogues, and would be thrown into prison. He knew that for witnessing to Him as the Messiah, some of them would suffer death. And something of this He told them. In speaking of their future, He was plain and definite, that in their coming trial they might remember His words and be strengthened to believe in Him as the Redeemer.

He spoke to them also words of hope and courage. "Let not your heart be troubled," He said; "ye believe in God, believe also in Me. In My Father's house are many mansions: if it were not so, I would have told you. I go to prepare a place for you. And if I go and prepare a place for you, I will come again, and receive you unto Myself; that where I am, there ye may be also. And whither I go ye know, and the way ye know." John 14:1-4. For your sake I came into the world; for you I have been working.

When I go away I shall still work earnestly for you. I came to the world to reveal Myself to you, that you might believe. I go to My Father and yours to co-operate with Him in your behalf.

"Verily, verily, I say unto you, He that believeth on Me, the works that I do shall he do also; and greater works than these shall he do; because I go unto My Father." John 14:12. By this, Christ did not mean that the disciples would make more exalted exertions than He had made, but that their work would have greater magnitude. He did not refer merely to miracle working, but to all that would take place under the agency of the Holy Spirit. "When the Comforter is come," He said, "whom I will send unto you from the Father, even the Spirit of truth, which proceedeth from the Father, He shall testify of Me: and ye also shall bear witness, because ye have been with Me from the beginning." John 15:26, 27.

Wonderfully were these words fulfilled. After the descent of the Holy Spirit, the disciples were so filled with love for Him and for those for whom He died, that hearts were melted by the words they spoke and the prayers they offered. They spoke in the power of the Spirit; and under the influence of that power, thousands were converted.

As Christ's representatives the apostles were to make a decided impression on the world. The fact that they were humble men would not diminish their influence, but increase it; for the minds of their hearers would be carried from them to the Saviour, who, though unseen, was still working with them. The wonderful teaching of the apostles, their words of courage and trust, would assure all that it was not in their own power that they worked, but in the power of Christ. Humbling themselves, they would declare that He whom the Jews had crucified was the Prince of life, the Son of the living God, and that in His name they did the works that He had done.

In His parting conversation with His disciples on the night before the crucifixion the Saviour made no reference to the suffering that He had endured and must yet endure. He did not speak of the humiliation that was before Him, but sought to bring to their minds that which would strengthen their faith, leading them to look forward to the joys that await the overcomer. He rejoiced in the consciousness that He could and would do more for His followers than He had promised; that from Him would flow forth love and compassion, cleansing the soul temple, and making men like Him in character; that His truth, armed with the power of the Spirit, would go forth conquering and to conquer.

"These things I have spoken unto you," He said, "that in Me ye might have peace. In the world ye shall have tribulation: but be of good cheer; I have overcome the world." John 16:33. Christ did not fail, neither was He discouraged; and the disciples were to show a faith of the same enduring nature. They were to work as He had worked, depending on Him for strength. Though their way would be obstructed by apparent impossibilities, yet by His grace they were to go forward, despairing of nothing and hoping for everything.

Christ had finished the work that was given Him to do. He had gathered out those who were to continue His work among men. And He said: "I am glorified in them. And now I am no more in the world, but these are in the world, and I come to Thee. Holy Father, keep through Thine own name those whom Thou hast given Me, that they may be one, as We are." "Neither pray I for these alone, but for them also which shall believe on Me through their word; that they all may be one; . . . I in them and Thou in Me, that they may be made perfect in one; and that the world may know that Thou hast sent Me, and hast loved them, as Thou hast loved Me." John 17:10, 11, 20-23.

# Assignments: Lesson 3

## The Tools of the Preacher's Trade

**Class Assignment:**
Attend the tutorial "The Tools of the Preacher's Trade" and read the related class notes.

**Reading Assignment:**
Charles E. Bradford, *Preaching to the Times*, Chapter 2, "Consider the Source."

**Reading**
Charles E. Bradford, *Preaching to the Times* 25-35.

"Consider the Source"

*For Ezra had set his heart to study the law of the Lord, and to do it, and to teach his statues and ordinances in Israel (Ezra 7:10, R.S.V.).*

In preaching we are dealing with ideas, concepts, facts, data, a whole universe of knowledge and thought. The preacher needs to know the sources from whence issue these ideas and concepts. He needs to know where to find the truths that transform and call men to decision. The man who stands to preach must have something to offer. His message, the goods he seeks to deliver through his preaching, comes from some source. What is it? Is it his own experience, out of his own head, the borrowed product of some other human mind? Preacher, just what is your source? The people have a right to know.

In the interest of the consumer the Federal Government is requiring manufacturers and producers to label their products. Food processors especially must tell the people what is in the package. Vitamins, minerals, calories, fat, and minimum daily requirements are what nutrition-minded homemakers are conscious of. Some even want to know whether it was organically grown.

How would our sermons stand up if tests were applied as to spiritual content and spiritual nutritional value? Again, it all depends on the source. We need a source that is authentic, accurate, and reliable.

Here is where the Seventh-day Adventist preacher is way out front. We acknowledge heartily that our primary sources are: (1) the Bible and (2) the Spirit of Prophecy. These are the norms whereby all else is tested. We acknowledge also that there are other sources: (1) the world of nature, (2) the product of men's minds (books), (3) our own experience in Christ.

Our first and best efforts should be given to the study of the primary sources. It seems almost unnecessary to say it, but say it I will at the risk of seeming prosaic, Seventh-day Adventist preachers need to study the Bible more. Please note I did not say study about the Bible.

Most of us have received the message second hand. We did not engage in that difficult mind-stretching investigation of biblical truth that brought out the specific doctrines and prophecies like links in a chain, those precious beliefs that make Adventism what it is. We received the package after it was put together.

The best thing that could happen to some of us would be to have every book in our libraries stolen for a while until we learned how to search the Scriptures.

Dr. Floyd Doud Shafer is using hyperbole and may seem a bit extreme, but we can all share his concern for the busy modern all-things-to-all-men pastor, when he says:

> Fling him into his office, tear the office sign from the door and nail on the sign, study. Take him off the mailing list, lock him up with . . . his typewriter and his Bible. . . . Shut his garrulous mouth spouting remarks and stop his tongue always tripping lightly over everything non-essential. Bend his knees to the lonesome valley, and fire him from the PTA and cancel his country club membership. Rip out his telephone, burn his ecclesiastical success sheets, refuse his glad hand, put water in the gas tank of his community buggy and compel him to be a minister of the Word.—Quoted in Gerald Kennedy, *The Seven Worlds of the Minister,* p. 95.

The Word of God needs to be read as a unit. It also needs to be read from various perspectives; as doctrine, as practical instruction, for inspiration, as history, and for spiritual comfort. It was to a preacher that Paul said, "All scripture is inspired by God and profitable for teaching, for reproof, for correction and for training in righteousness, that the man of God may be complete, equipped for every good work" (2 Tim. 3:16, R.S.V.).

The Bible must be something more to the preacher than a hunting ground for texts, it must be food for his own soul. Halford Luccock says:

> The fruitful reading of the Bible, is a sort of brooding, not frantic reading; rather it is watching the narrative pass before one's mind, holding the mind loose, with no tension or tautness at all, not worrying whether one finds anything or not. The key point is that one is not working for a particular end. The mind broods over the page like a hawk over a chicken yard; then, from a leisurely wheel in the air, it swoops down on what looks like an idea. You don't always get a live chicken. Sometimes it turns out to be merely a hole in the ground. Don't fret about that. The chief thing is the habit, the procedure.—*In the Minister's Workshop,* p. 160.

The preacher must be able to declare what he has personally found. "Thy words were found, and I ate them, and thy words became to me a joy and the delight of my heart" (Jer. 15:16, R.S.V.).

P. T. Forsyth was talking to preachers about their preaching when he said, "You do not yet know the inner Christ who are but His lovers or friends. You need to have been His patient and to owe Him your life."—P. T. Forsyth, *Positive Preaching*, p. 190.

As the spiritual has it:

"When I was sick, Lord, You healed me,

When I was down, Lord, You raised me;

When I was hungry, You fed me,

And I just thank You all the days of my life."

For a change try the inductive method of Bible study. Get a book like *Methodical Bible Study*, by Robert A. Traina, and the little companion volume *The Joy of Discovery*, by Oletta Wald. This approach to Bible study is helpful in that it increases the powers of observation. It is difficult to argue with Oletta Wald when she says:

> In . . . [the methodical approach] you follow an orderly and logical pattern as you study your Bible lessons. . . . Method is as important in Bible study as it is in farming or baking. As a Bible student, if you develop an orderly and logical procedure in your study, you will gain more insight and receive much greater satisfaction than if you proceed in a hit and miss fashion.—*The Joy of Discovery*, p. 6.

Here is a profitable exercise. Take your *Index to the Writings of Ellen G. White* and look at the references under Scripture, Students of, Study (investigation or searching). These two sub-headings take up six pages. I picked out a few almost at random. First under *Students:* "Ministers should be close," *Testimonies,* vol. 2, p. 499; "gospel workers should be," *ibid.*, vol. 5, p. 592; "should learn to view God's Word as a whole," *Evangelism*, p. 399; "should see relationship to their parts," *ibid.*, p. 399; "richest treasures of thought await skillful and diligent," *Counsels to Teachers*, p. 461. Next under *Study:* "Ministers should not neglect careful," *Testimonies*, vol. 4, p. 380; "verse by verse method often most helpful," *Education*, p. 189; "diligent research and continuous effort needed in," *ibid.*, p. 123; "engage in both for doctrinal and practical lessons," *Sons and Daughters of God*, p. 279; "should guard jealously hours for," *Gospel Workers*, p. 100; "as miners digging for gold," *Fundamentals of Christian Education*, p. 307; "vigor of mind given by," *Medical Ministry*, p. 294; "with fasting and prayer," *Testimonies*, vol. 2,

p. 692; "young men need for themselves," *Testimonies to Ministers*, p. 109.

A man who studies his Bible prayerfully, thoughtfully, regularly, and systematically will build up a reservoir. He will find himself preaching out the overflow.

I find myself in complete agreement with James S. Stewart, when he says:

> Again and again in your reading of the Bible, phrases, sentences, whole passages will leap out from the page, each of them positively thrusting itself upon you, and clamoring "One day you must preach on me!" This is where your private notebooks come into action. When a text has once gripped you, do not let it escape. Jot it down at the head of a page, and underneath it any thoughts, illustrations, potential sermon divisions it may have brought with it. There is a tragic page in the biography of Hector Berlioz the composer, which tells how one night there came to him quite suddenly an inspiration for a new symphony. The theme of the first movement, an Allegro, was ringing in his head: he knew he ought to capture it there and then, and set the music down in manuscript, but he refrained. The following night it returned, and again he heard the Allegro clearly, and sang it to himself, and even seemed to see it written down: but again he failed to take his pen. The next day, when he awoke, all remembrance of it was gone: the lovely melody refused to be recaptured, and the symphony which might have thrilled the world was never written. Let that sad episode be a warning.—*Heralds of God*, p. 154.

After the Bible, our other primary source is the writings of Ellen G. White. These writings are without peer when it comes to illuminating and amplifying the Scriptures. What a soul-building adventure it would be to read the Bible and the Conflict of the Ages books concurrently! A man's preaching would have to benefit.

I have a friend who undertook the ambitious task of reading his Bible and *The SDA Bible Commentary* through in a single year. He was immeasurably enriched by his task and his preaching showed it.

Just as the Seventh-day Adventist preacher must develop a hermeneutic for the Bible, so he must develop one for the Spirit of Prophecy. While the Greeks were people of the eye, the Jews were people of the ear. We need to develop what someone has called charismatic hearing. There is a voice in the Bible, there is a voice in the writings of Ellen G. White.

One of Jesus' favorite expressions was, "If any man has ears to hear, let him hear." In one of His discourses He continues—

> "Take heed what you hear; the measure you give will be the measure you get, and still more will be given you. For to him who has more will be given; and from him who has not, even what he has will be taken away" (Mark 4:24, 25, R.S.V.).

It will take discipline to train the ear to hear, but it will pay off big dividends. D. T. Niles, the Indian churchman, put it beautifully:

> The Bible is written by men who were engaged in a conversation with God, and they wrote down what they heard God say about things that God had done and promised to do. When we read the Bible, we simply join in that conversation. We join in the conversation between God and Abraham, or God and David, or Jesus and the men on the road to Emmaus. In other words, the Bible speaks today because Jesus Christ has risen from the dead. That is the ongoing conversation. We join in the conversation on the road to Emmaus, and as we listen to Him as He talks, the words of Scripture become His words to us. So if the Bible is to speak today, it speaks to men who are engaged in conversation with the risen Christ.—*ABS Bulletin*, December, 1972.

Ellen White is speaking of the secondary sources when she says:

> The knowledge current in the world may be acquired; for all men are God's property, and are worked by God to fulfill His will in certain lines, even when they refuse the man Christ Jesus as their Saviour. The way in which God uses men is not always discerned, but He does use them. God intrusts men with talents and inventive genius, in order that His great work in our world may be accomplished.—*Fundamentals of Christian Education*, p. 409.

Set up a reading program to include fields of study other than your own. Take a little excursion into astronomy or the life sciences, as biology is now called. The big question for the busy Seventh-day Adventist preacher is How can I find time for all this? You must make it and take it. Keep some good reading material at hand. In order to keep up and not waste time in wading through trivia, join a good book club, check the book reviews in professional journals, correspond with men who read widely. When you do get a good book, make your own index on the blank pages in the back of the book as you read it through. I got this hint from W. E. Sangster, the great English preacher and teacher of preachers. You will thus be gathering up the fragments so that nothing will be lost. Even if you don't get to put it on index cards and file it away properly, at least you have noted it down. Remember, it is better to master a few books than skim through a vast library.

> Clearly, then, the preacher will be that rarest of men—a thinker. He will not be just a wide reader, peddling other people's thoughts. After his devotions, the best hour of his day will be the hour given to sheer thinking: assembling the facts, facing their apparent contradiction, reaching up for the help of God and, then, driving his brain like a bulldozer through the apparent chaos to order and understanding at the last.—W. E. Sangster, *The Craft of Sermon Construction*, p. 157.

Mastery of the sources, brethren, is prerequisite to effective preaching. Every one of us needs to establish a pattern of general and specific reading. We need to take time to do some hard theological thinking. And do commit portions of Scripture and the Spirit of Prophecy to memory. We must do this lest we become part of that "race of clerical visionaries" that Phillips Brooks spoke about, "who think vast, dim, vague thoughts and do no work." (He took his text and it took him.) Or fall under the class indicated by Ernest Fremont Tittle when he said, "Too many preachers are laying down on the job. . . . The time which they do spend among their books, so to speak more accurately, in the same room with their books—what do they do with it? Mostly they kill it."

One of the black fathers, M. G. Nunez, had a name for these ministerial drones—"tithe eaters." God forbid that the appellation fits us.

Charles W. Koller in his book *Expository Preaching Without Notes* is on target when he says:

> A preacher will not long hold the interest of his people if he preaches only "out of the fullness of his heart and the emptiness of his head." The pastor must reckon with the probability of having to prepare about one hundred and fifty messages a year, including Sundays, Wednesdays, funeral services and special occasions. This adds up to an enormous output. The only safeguard against poverty of thought is by way of constant exposure to the sources of preaching material, and constant replenishment from these sources. Laying up resources is a matter of years of sustained effort and meditation. Sermons are developed more or less unconsciously, and there is no substitute for the prolonged general preparation behind the immediate specific preparation.—Page 44.

Don't fall into the habit of studying for sermons alone. As P. T. Forsyth said, "Read at fountainheads." We may never become great systematic theologians, but we are for all of that practical theologians, because there can be no divorce between theology and preaching. Every pastor is a theologian in residence. Preaching is a sort of immediate theologizing. And, remember, if it won't preach, it's not good theology.

What are the fountainheads at which the Seventh-day Adventist preacher must fill his cup? *Revelation/Inspiration* and its streams and branches: divine communication, prophecy, history. *Christology and the Godhead:* angels and demons, Paul's principalities and powers. S*oteriology:* Creation and the Fall, the nature of man, the law of God, sin, the plan of redemption, atonement, eschatology, apocalypticism. *Ecclesiology*, and all that subsumes under this great division: God's purpose for man, the kingdom of God, the nature of the church, the church as servant, spiritual gifts, mission, the lordship of Christ, et cetera. But it has fallen to modern church to have its problem focus on ecclesiology.

The gospel minister is urged to diligently gather up the jewels of truth, and place them in the *framework* of the gospel (see *Gospel Workers*, p. 289). The preacher should have this framework fully developed. I don't like the term "systematic theology" too much, because in some circles it suggest a sort of philosophical approach to theology apart from biblical revelation. Nevertheless, our theology must have system, that firmly established framework that Ellen White speaks about. After the framework is set, we can begin the lifelong task of discovery and recovery of these jewels that are "scattered over the field of revelation" (*Fundamentals of Christian Education*, p. 188).

Studying at fountainheads will help the preacher develop a world view, get back to the sources of theological thought, see the broad spectrum of truth and the relationship between its main branches. It will help him to avoid riding hobby horses and exalting minor matters as major doctrines.

Every heresy that has plagued the church came as a result of the failure of capable men to read and study at fountainheads, and also because they developed their theology in a vacuum without reference to the corrective influence of their peers and the tested thinking and convictions of their spiritual forebears.

We shall not go wrong if we are guided by Ellen White's counsel:

> The passing of the time in 1844 was a period of great events, opening to our astonished eyes the cleansing of the sanctuary transpiring in heaven, and having decided relation to God's people upon the earth, [also] the first and second angels' messages and the third, unfurling the banner on which was inscribed, "The commandments of God and the faith of Jesus." One of the landmarks under this message was the temple of God, seen by His truth-loving people in heaven, and the ark containing the law of God. The light of the Sabbath of the fourth commandment flashed its strong rays in the pathway of the transgressors of God's law. The nonimmortality of the wicked is an old landmark. I can call to mind nothing more that can come under the head of the old landmarks. All this cry about changing the old landmarks is all imaginary.—*Counsels to Writers and Editors*, pp. 30, 31.

Theology is still the queen of the sciences because it alone can answer the ultimate questions—origin, identity, and destiny.

And biblical preaching makes available to our people this knowledge of God, which is found most clearly in the Scriptures. Biblical preaching is the need of the hour. The parish preacher is the middleman who must take the thousand-dollar bills of academic theology and change them into the coin of the realm so that his people can make use of it in the market place of life.

There has been a swing toward psychological, personal-problem preaching in the Adventist Church of recent date. This was to be expected as a normal reaction to the heavy diet of doctrinal/prophetic preaching of the thirties and forties. Great public evangelism campaigns were the order of the day, with large accessions to the faith. Since that time the intelligence level, or to state it more accurately, the education level, of pulpit and pew has risen sharply. We suddenly discovered man, his problems, hangups, et cetera. The Adventist community looked at itself critically for perhaps the first time. We began to hear arguments something like this: doctrine must be related to life. Just to know the 2300 days is not enough. Something more is needed. The academicians warned the preachers: your churches are full of problems. Your people need more than the usual Sabbath sermon, totally unrelated to life situations. A better-educated clergy agreed, and the swing was on.

I am not knocking sermons whose thrust is toward problem-solving. I am against any approach to preaching that tends to become man-centered. There is a certain attraction in humanism, a subtle appeal in the new psychology or behavioral science. It is exciting to discover what makes man tick. Over and against the gloomy Puritan ethic, with its angry God and helpless man, Freud and Jung do have their appeal. But the swing may now have gone too far.

Today we have a whole new church audience. Most of them have never been through a long evangelistic campaign (three-week campaigns have been in for some time) and heard the full treatment of those special truths that make us a church separate and distinct. We must not take for granted that they know. With an increase in general literacy, there seems to be a corresponding decrease in Biblical literacy. It is seen even in our children who have gone through our school system. In these critical times there must be no neglect of the *didache* function of our pulpit ministry.

My plea is for biblical preaching, not sterile recitation of propositionally stated truths in the old rabbinic tradition. The task of the Seventh-day Adventist ministry today is to take these truths, make them come alive, demonstrate their relation to life and how they meet contemporary issues and human needs. The message is still present truth. Under the ministration of the Holy Spirit old truths can flash forth with new relevance. Skillful biblical preaching releases the dynamic that is in the Word, and scripture once again becomes profitable for "teaching the truth and refuting error, or for reformation of manners and discipline in right living" (2 Tim. 3:16, N.E.B.).

To lighten up our discussion a bit: "In those days quite a number of Apolloses, on graduating (for there were few university grads among us) having become men, put away such childish things as texts and Bible stories. In the pulpit they showed great knowledge of Freud and Jung and Adler. Then after a while, having explored man's psyche and diagnosed his problems quite eruditely, like the prodigal son they began to be in want. Then they came to themselves and said, 'In our Father's house [the remnant church] there are truths enough and to spare,' and they said, 'I will arise and go back to the Bible.'" (Apologies to Halford Luccock.)

It is true that there is a renewed interest in, and heart cry for, strong biblical preaching among us. Wise preachers will recognize it.

> The hearts of many in the world as well as many church members are hungering for the bread of life and thirsting for the waters of salvation. They are interested in the service of song, but they are not longing for that or even prayer. They want to know the Scriptures. What saith the Word of God to me? The Holy Spirit is working on mind and heart, drawing them to the bread of life. They see everything around them changing. Human feelings, human ideas of what constitutes religion, change. They come to hear the Word just as it reads.—*Evangelism*, p. 501.

I am struck by Ellen G. White's accurate reading of the situation. People today are reaching out for a biblical explanation of life and biblical clues to the meaning of the times. This renewed interest in the Bible is especially manifest among young people both in the Adventist community and the community at large.

A recent study conducted by Douglas W. Johnson and George W. Cornell is significant. Contrary to the predictions of the secular theologians, "the strong, steady note that sounded throughout this study was the overwhelming, unshaken dedication to classic Christian beliefs, a plea for fuller teaching of them, and an insistence that they be plainly proclaimed in the cause of evangelizing the nations and winning others to faith in Christ."—*Punctured Preconceptions*, p. 188.

Notice how Ellen White speaks of the universal need, the heart cry of many in the world and in the church, "for the bread of life." This is precisely why biblical preaching is so rewarding. Human needs are met, not only on the surface but at deepest levels of existence. And if the word preached in our churches speaks to the vital needs of church members that same word will speak to the needs of those outside our ranks.

My recent contacts with young people reinforce the conviction that biblical preaching is "in." The question that surfaces over and over again is: "How can I come to grips with Bible study? Can you give me some hints as to how Bible study can be more fulfilling and satisfying on a personal basis?" I get this from new Christians, those of mature Christian experience, and even those who appear only casually interested in religion. They seem to sense that the Bible has something to say about life, the meaning of existence on this planet, but somehow it remains out of reach. To many the Book is like a safe filled with treasure. What they want to know is the combination, how to unlock the storehouse.

Jesus' words speak with tremendous relevance to the modern preacher. "Every scribe which is instructed unto the kingdom of heaven is like unto a man that is an householder, which bringeth forth out of his treasure things new and old" (Matt. 13:52).

This leads me to conclude that Bible study—good old-fashioned, first-hand Bible study—should be our first work. We should bring to this exercise the very highest powers of the intellect.

*On Reading Non-Seventh-day Adventist Authors.* There was a time when the question was raised as to the value of reading non-Seventh-day Adventist authors per se. Few would raise the question today. It is evident that Ellen White read Bunyan, Baxter, and a number of her contemporaries. But the question still remains, to what extent should these men be read?

It is clear that we will derive no good from reading authors whose writings are patently negative, based upon "infidel philosophies," who cast aspersion on Christ's gospel. (You will find excellent guidelines in the Spirit of Prophecy.) But we must also recognize that God does work also through other minds than those that are among us. There are some men who are searching for truth, struggling for insights. We need to know their thinking, what routes they are taking in their search. The Adventist preacher should know what is going on in the theological world. What are the straws in the wind? The Lord's messenger was clear in her own thinking as to the value of "a knowledge of theology as taught in the leading institutions of learning" in preparing young men to "labor for the educated classes and to meet the prevailing errors of our time" (*Testimonies*, vol. 5, p. 584).

It is helpful to know the trends in the various theological camps to note points of agreement and disagreement. It is my conviction that Seventh-day Adventists cannot identify too closely with any wing of Protestantism, liberal, conservative, or fundamental. For instance, we are closer to the recent position of many liberals on the state of the dead and the nonimmortality of the soul.

Without being too rigid it can be stated this way: (1) We do not read non Seventh day Adventist authors to discover and formulate a system of truth. However, (2) there may be some supportive elements in various points of view. Thus, (3) helpful findings from outside sources should be referred to our already established system. (4) Such authors should be sampled. But the steady diet should be derived from our own sources.

It may be helpful to note here that our system was not developed by any one great theologian. It is not identified by any one big name. There is no dominant, overpowering figure. In the providence of God this has proved a distinct advantage. Our system of truth was not worked out privately, cannot be labeled and categorized, does not rise and fall on one man. It is not static or bound by creedal statements. In the mind of our prophet it was always to be dynamic, ongoing, and open-ended toward development.

Really the Seventh-day Adventist pulpit is the freest in Christendom. We have no lectionary, no society for the propagation of the faith, no index or inquisition. The charge to the Seventh-day Adventist preacher is simply, "Preach the word." Room is left for the Spirit to lead, and because He is resident in the whole church, light and truth may come from any source. This is why only responsible persons should be given the forum of an Adventist pulpit. This is why the spirit of the preacher is as important as his theology. It takes a certain type of man to discern the fine line that separates liberty from license and to respect it!

# Assignments: Lesson 4

## Deciding What to Preach

**Class assignment:**
Attend the tutorial "Deciding What to Preach" and read the related class notes.

**Reading assignment:**
E. G. White, *Christ's Object Lessons*, "Talents" (portion).

**Written assignment:**
From your reading of the chapter on "Talents" from *Christ's Object Lessons*, select any paragraph that you feel says something you needed to learn and write out in full a short talk (8-10 minutes in length) in which you explain what you learned and how this will affect your approach to lay preaching. Submit a written version of this talk and be prepared to present it orally to the class.

**Reading**
Ellen G. White, *Christ's Object Lessons* 325-333 and 335-339.

"Talents"

Christ on the Mount of Olives had spoken to His disciples of His second advent to the world. He had specified certain signs that were to show when His coming was near, and had bidden His disciples watch and be ready. Again He repeated the warning, "Watch therefore; for ye know neither the day nor the hour wherein the Son of man cometh." Then He showed what it means to watch for His coming. The time is to be spent, not in idle waiting, but in diligent working. This lesson He taught in the parable of the talents.

"The kingdom of heaven," He said, "is as a man traveling into a far country, who called his own servants, and delivered unto them his goods. And unto one he gave five talents, to another two, and to another one; to every man according to his several ability; and straightway took his journey."

The man traveling into a far country represents Christ, who, when speaking this parable, was soon to depart from this earth to heaven. The "bondservants" (R. V.), or slaves, of the parable, represent the followers of Christ. We are not our own. We have been "bought with a price" (1 Cor. 6:20), not "with corruptible things, as silver and gold, . . . but with the precious blood of Christ" (1 Peter 1:18, 19); "that they which live should not henceforth live unto themselves, but unto Him which died for them, and rose again" (2 Cor. 5:15).

All men have been bought with this infinite price. By pouring the whole treasury of heaven into this world, by giving us in Christ all heaven, God has purchased the will, the affections, the mind, the soul, of every human being. Whether believers or unbelievers, all men are the Lord's property. All are called to do service for Him, and for the manner in which they have met this claim, all will be required to render an account at the great judgment day.

But the claims of God are not recognized by all. It is those who profess to have accepted Christ's service who in the parable are represented as His own servants.

Christ's followers have been redeemed for service. Our Lord teaches that the true object of life is ministry. Christ Himself was a worker, and to all His followers He gives the law of service—service to God and to their fellow men. Here Christ has presented to the world a higher conception of life than they had ever known. By living to minister for others, man is brought into connection with Christ. The law of service becomes the connecting link which binds us to God and to our fellow men.

To His servants Christ commits "His goods"—something to be put to use for Him. He gives "to every man his work." Each has his place in the eternal plan of heaven. Each is to work in cooperation with Christ for the salvation of souls. Not more surely is the place prepared for us in the heavenly mansions than is the special place designated on earth where we are to work for God.

**Gifts of the Holy Spirit**

The talents that Christ entrusts to His church represent especially the gifts and blessings imparted by the Holy Spirit. "To one is given by the Spirit the word of wisdom; to another the word of knowledge by the same Spirit; to another faith by the same Spirit; to another the gifts of healing by the same Spirit; to another the working of miracles; to another prophecy; to another discerning of spirits; to another divers kinds of tongues; to another the interpretation of tongues: but all these worketh that one and the selfsame Spirit, dividing to every man severally as He will." 1 Cor. 12:8-11. All men do not receive the same gifts, but to every servant of the Master some gift of the Spirit is promised.

Before He left His disciples, Christ "breathed on them, and saith unto them, Receive ye the Holy Ghost." John 20:22. Again He said, "Behold, I send the promise of My Father upon you." Luke 24:29. But not until after the ascension was the gift received in its fullness. Not until through faith and prayer the disciples had surrendered themselves fully for His working was the outpouring of the Spirit received. Then in a special sense the goods of heaven were committed to the followers of Christ. "When He ascended up on high, He led captivity captive, and gave gifts unto men." Eph. 4:8, 7. "Unto every one of us is given grace, according to the measure of the gift of Christ," the Spirit "dividing to every man severally as He will." 1 Cor. 12:11. The gifts are already ours in Christ, but their actual possession depends upon our reception of the Spirit of God.

The promise of the Spirit is not appreciated as it should be. Its fulfillment is not realized as it might be. It is the absence of the Spirit that makes the gospel ministry so powerless. Learning, talents, eloquence, every natural or acquired endowment, may be possessed; but without the presence of the Spirit of God, no heart will be touched, no sinner be won to Christ. On the other hand, if they are connected with Christ, if the gifts of the Spirit are theirs, the poorest and most ignorant of His disciples will have a power that will tell upon hearts. God makes them the channel for the outworking of the highest influence in the universe.

**Other Talents**

The special gifts of the Spirit are not the only talents represented in the parable. It includes all gifts and endowments, whether original or acquired, natural or spiritual. All are to be employed in Christ's service. In becoming His disciples, we surrender ourselves to Him with all that we are and have. These gifts He returns to us purified and ennobled, to be used for His glory in blessing our fellow men.

To every man God has given "according to his several ability." The talents are not apportioned capriciously. He who has ability to use five talents receives five. He who can improve but two, receives two. He who can wisely use only one, receives one. None need lament that they have not received larger gifts; for He who has apportioned to every man is equally honored by the improvement of each trust, whether it be great or small. The one to whom five talents have been committed is to render the improvement of five; he who has but one, the improvement of one. God expects returns "according to that a man hath, and not according to that he hath not." 2 Cor. 8:12.

**Use of Talents**

In the parable he that had "received the five talents went and traded with the same, and made them other five talents; and likewise he that had received two, he also gained other two."

The talents, however few, are to be put to use. The question that most concerns us is not, How much have I received? but, What am I doing with that which I have? The development of all our powers is the first duty we owe to God and to our fellow men. No one who is not growing daily in capability and usefulness is fulfilling the purpose of life. In making a profession of faith in Christ we pledge ourselves to become all that it is possible for us to be as workers for the Master, and we should cultivate every faculty to the highest degree of perfection, that we may do the greatest amount of good of which we are capable.

The Lord has a great work to be done, and He will bequeath the most in the future life to those who do the most faithful, willing service in the present life. The Lord chooses His own agents, and each day under different circumstances He gives them a trial in His plan of operation. In each true-hearted endeavor to work out His plan, He chooses His agents not because they are perfect but because, through a connection with Him, they may gain perfection.

God will accept only those who are determined to aim high. He places every human agent under obligation to do his best. Moral perfection is required of all. Never should we lower the standard of righteousness in order to accommodate inherited or cultivated tendencies to wrongdoing. We need to understand that imperfection of character is sin. All righteous attributes of character dwell in God as a perfect, harmonious whole, and every one who receives Christ as a personal Saviour is privileged to possess these attributes.

And those who would be workers together with God must strive for perfection of every organ of the body and quality of the mind. True education is the preparation of the physical, mental, and moral powers for the performance of every duty; it is the training of body, mind, and soul for divine service. This is the education that will endure unto eternal life.

Of every Christian the Lord requires growth in efficiency and capability in every line. Christ has paid us our wages, even His own blood and suffering, to secure our willing service. He came to our world to give us an example of how we should work, and what spirit we should bring into our labor. He desires us to study how we can best advance His work and glorify His name in the world, crowning with honor, with the greatest love and devotion, the Father who "so loved the world, that He gave His only begotten Son, that whosoever believeth in Him should not perish, but have everlasting life." John 3:16.

But Christ has given us no assurance that to attain perfection of character is an easy matter. A noble, all-round character is not inherited. It does not come to us by accident. A noble character is earned by individual effort through the merits and grace of Christ. God gives the talents, the powers of the mind; we form the character. It is formed by hard, stern battles with self. Conflict after conflict must be waged against hereditary tendencies. We shall have to criticize ourselves closely, and allow not one unfavorable trait to remain uncorrected.

Let no one say, I cannot remedy my defects of character. If you come to this decision, you will certainly fail of obtaining everlasting life. The impossibility lies in your own will. If you will not, then you can not overcome. The real difficulty arises from the corruption of an unsanctified heart, and an unwillingness to submit to the control of God.

Many whom God has qualified to do excellent work accomplish very little, because they attempt little. Thousands pass through life as if they had no definite object for which to live, no standard to reach. Such will obtain a reward proportionate to their works.

Remember that you will never reach a higher standard than you yourself set. Then set your mark high, and step by step, even though it be by painful effort, by self-denial and sacrifice, ascend the whole length of the ladder of progress. Let nothing hinder you. Fate has not woven its meshes about any human being so firmly that he need remain helpless and in uncertainty. Opposing circumstances should create a firm determination to overcome them. The breaking down of one barrier will give greater ability and courage to go forward. Press with determination in the right direction, and circumstances will be your helpers, not your hindrances.

Be ambitious, for the Master's glory, to cultivate every grace of character. In every phase of your character building you are to please God. This you may do; for Enoch pleased Him though living in a degenerate age. And there are Enochs in this our day.

Stand like Daniel, that faithful statesman, a man whom no temptation could corrupt. Do not disappoint Him who so loved you that He gave His own life to cancel your sins. He says, "Without Me ye can do nothing." John 15:5. Remember this. If you have made mistakes, you certainly gain a victory if you see these mistakes and regard them as beacons of warning. Thus you turn defeat into victory, disappointing the enemy and honoring your Redeemer.

A character formed according to the divine likeness is the only treasure that we can take from this world to the next. Those who are under the instruction of Christ in this world will take every divine attainment with them to the heavenly mansions. And in heaven we are continually to improve. How important, then, is the development of character in this life.

The heavenly intelligences will work with the human agent who seeks with determined faith that perfection of character which will reach out to perfection in action. To everyone engaged in this work Christ says, I am at your right hand to help you.

As the will of man co-operates with the will of God, it becomes omnipotent. Whatever is to be done at His command may be accomplished in His strength. All His biddings are enablings.

\* \* \*

## Speech

The power of speech is a talent that should be diligently cultivated. Of all the gifts we have received from God, none is capable of being a greater blessing than this. With the voice we convince and persuade, with it we offer prayer and praise to God, and with it we tell others of the Redeemer's love. How important, then, that it be so trained as to be most effective for good.

The culture and right use of the voice are greatly neglected, even by persons of intelligence and Christian activity. There are many who read or speak in so low or so rapid a manner that they cannot be readily understood. Some have a thick, indistinct utterance; others speak in a high key, in sharp, shrill tones, that are painful to the hearers. Texts, hymns, and the reports and other papers presented before public assemblies are sometimes read in such a way that they are not understood and often so that their force and impressiveness are destroyed.

This is an evil that can and should be corrected. On this point the Bible gives instruction. Of the Levites who read the Scriptures to the people in the days of Ezra, it is said, "They read in the book in the law of God distinctly, and gave the sense, and caused them to understand the reading." Neh. 8:8.

By diligent effort all may acquire the power to read intelligibly, and to speak in a full, clear, round tone, in a distinct and impressive manner. By doing this we may greatly increase our efficiency as workers for Christ.

Every Christian is called to make known to others the unsearchable riches of Christ; therefore he should seek for perfection in speech. He should present the word of God in a way that will commend it to the hearers. God does not design that His human channels shall be uncouth. It is not His will that man shall belittle or degrade the heavenly current that flows through him to the world.

We should look to Jesus, the perfect pattern; we should pray for the aid of the Holy Spirit, and in His strength we should seek to train every organ for perfect work.

Especially is this true of those who are called to public service. Every minister and every teacher should bear in mind that he is giving to the people a message that involves eternal interests. The truth spoken will judge them in the great day of final reckoning. And with some souls the manner of the one delivering the message will determine its reception or rejection. Then let the word be so spoken that it will appeal to the understanding and impress the heart. Slowly, distinctly, and solemnly should it be spoken, yet with all the earnestness which its importance demands.

The right culture and use of the power of speech has to do with every line of Christian work; it enters into the home life, and into all our intercourse with one another. We should accustom ourselves to speak in pleasant tones, to use pure and correct language, and words that are kind and courteous. Sweet, kind words are as dew and gentle showers to the soul. The Scripture says of Christ that grace was poured into His lips that He might "know how to speak a word in season to him that is weary." Ps. 45:2; Isa. 50:4. And the Lord bids us, "Let your speech be always with grace" (Col. 4:6) "that it may minister grace unto the hearers" (Eph. 4:29).

In seeking to correct or reform others we should be careful of our words. They will be a savor of life unto life or of death unto death. In giving reproof or counsel, many indulge in sharp, severe speech, words not adapted to heal the wounded soul. By these ill-advised expressions the spirit is chafed, and often the erring ones are stirred to rebellion. All who would advocate the principles of truth need to receive the heavenly oil of love. Under all circumstances reproof should be spoken in love. Then our words will reform but not exasperate. Christ by His Holy Spirit will supply the force and the power. This is His work.

Not one word is to be spoken unadvisedly. No evil speaking, no frivolous talk, no fretful repining or impure suggestion, will escape the lips of him who is following Christ. The apostle Paul, writing by the Holy Spirit, says, "Let no corrupt communication proceed out of your mouth." Eph. 4:29. A corrupt communication does not mean only words that are vile. It means any expression contrary to holy principles and pure and undefiled religion. It includes impure hints and covert insinuations of evil. Unless instantly resisted, these lead to great sin.

Upon every family, upon every individual Christian, is laid the duty of barring the way against corrupt speech. When in the company of those who indulge in foolish talk, it is our duty to change the subject of conversation if possible. By the help of the grace of God we should quietly drop words or introduce a subject that will turn the conversation into a profitable channel.

It is the work of parents to train their children to proper habits of speech. The very best school for this culture is the home life. From the earliest years the children should be taught to speak respectfully and lovingly to their parents and to one another. They should be taught that only words of gentleness, truth, and purity must pass their lips. Let the parents themselves be daily learners in the school of Christ. Then by precept and example they can teach their children the use of "sound speech, that cannot be condemned." Titus 2:8. This is one of the greatest and most responsible of their duties.

As followers of Christ we should make our words such as to be a help and an encouragement to one another in the Christian life. Far more than we do, we need to speak of the precious chapters in our experience. We should speak of the mercy and loving-kindness of God, of the matchless depths of the Saviour's love. Our words should be words of praise and thanksgiving. If the mind and heart are full of the love of God, this will be revealed in the conversation. It will not be a difficult matter to impart that which enters into our spiritual life. Great thoughts, noble aspirations, clear perceptions of truth, unselfish purposes, yearnings for piety and holiness, will bear fruit in words that reveal the character of the heart treasure. When Christ is thus revealed in our speech, it will have power in winning souls to Him.

We should speak of Christ to those who know Him not. We should do as Christ did. Wherever He was, in the synagogue, by the wayside, in the boat thrust out a little from the land, at the Pharisee's feast or the table of the publican, He spoke to men of the things pertaining to the higher life. The things of nature, the events of daily life, were bound up by Him with the words of truth. The hearts of His hearers were drawn to Him; for He had healed their sick, had comforted their sorrowing ones, and had taken their children in His arms and blessed them. When He opened His lips to speak, their attention was riveted upon Him, and every word was to some soul a savor of life unto life.

So it should be with us. Wherever we are, we should watch for opportunities of speaking to others of the Saviour. If we follow Christ's example in doing good, hearts will open to us as they did to Him. Not abruptly, but with tact born of divine love, we can tell them of Him who is the "Chiefest among ten thousand" and the One "altogether lovely." Cant. 5:10, 16. This is the very highest work in which we can employ the talent of speech. It was given to us that we might present Christ as the sin-pardoning Saviour.

# Assignments: Lesson 5

## Variety—The Spice of Sermons

**Class assignment:**
Attend the tutorial "Variety—The Spice of Sermons" and read the related class notes.

**Written assignment:**
Imagine that you are to preach at morning worship, in the same church, once per month for the next six months. Think specifically of the membership and attendance of your own congregation, of their real but varied needs, and of the themes the pastor and others are presently addressing on Sabbath mornings. Sketch a draft of subjects that you might use over the next six months which would supplement and provide breadth and balance for the listener.

# Assignments: Lesson 6

## Sermon Structure

**Class assignment:**
Attend the tutorial "Sermon Structure" and read the related class notes.

**Reading assignment:**
Study the sermon preached by Stephen before the Sanhedrin (Acts 7:1-53).

**Written assignment:**
Analyze Stephen's sermon before the Sanhedrin. Identify his introduction. Note how swiftly he moves into the body of his address. What is his main theme? How does he use illustrations? Study his conclusion. Why do you find it compelling?

# Assignments: Lesson 7

## Persuasive Preaching

**Class assignment:**

Attend the tutorial "Persuasive Preaching" and read the related class notes.

**Reading assignment:**

E. G. White, *The Desire of Ages,* Chapter 73 (portion), "Let Not Your Heart Be Troubled."

Acts 21:37 to 22:21; 24:10 to 24:21; 26:2 to 26:28.

**Written assignment:**

Consider the five elements of persuasive preaching: Passion, Relevance, Cohesion, Planned Psychology, and Clarity. Which of these five elements can you find in Paul's defense to King Agrippa in Acts 26? Give examples to demonstrate.

**Reading**

Ellen G. White, *The Desire of Ages* 668-772.

"Let Not Your Heart Be Troubled"

The Lord is disappointed when His people place a low estimate upon themselves. He desires His chosen heritage to value themselves according to the price He has placed upon them. God wanted them, else He would not have sent His Son on such an expensive errand to redeem them. He has a use for them, and He is well pleased when they make the very highest demands upon Him, that they may glorify His name. They may expect large things if they have faith in His promises.

But to pray in Christ's name means much. It means that we are to accept His character, manifest His spirit, and work His works. The Saviour's promise is given on condition. "If ye love Me," He says, "keep My commandments." He saves men, not in sin, but from sin; and those who love Him will show their love by obedience.

All true obedience comes from the heart. It was heart work with Christ. And if we consent, He will so identify Himself with our thoughts and aims, so blend our hearts and minds into conformity to His will, that when obeying Him we shall be but carrying out our own impulses. The will, refined and sanctified, will find its highest delight in doing His service. When we know God as it is our privilege to know, our life will be a life of continual obedience. Through an appreciation of the character of Christ, through communion with God, sin will become hateful to us.

As Christ lived the law in humanity, so we may do if we will take hold of the Strong for strength. But we are not to place the responsibility of our duty upon others, and wait for them to tell us what to do. We cannot depend for counsel upon humanity. The Lord will teach us our duty just as willingly as He will teach somebody else. If we come to Him in faith, He will speak His mysteries to us personally. Our hearts will often burn within us as One draws nigh to commune with us as He did with Enoch. Those who decide to do nothing in any line that will displease God, will know, after presenting their case before Him, just what course to pursue. And they will receive not only wisdom, but strength. Power for obedience, for service, will be imparted to them, as Christ has promised. Whatever was given to Christ—the "all things" to supply the need of fallen men—was given to Him as the head and representative of humanity. And "whatsoever we ask, we receive of Him, because we keep His commandments, and do those things that are pleasing in His sight." 1 John 3:22.

Before offering Himself as the sacrificial victim, Christ sought for the most essential and complete gift to bestow upon His followers, a gift that would bring within their reach the boundless resources of grace. "I will pray the Father," He said, "and He shall give you another Comforter, that He may abide with you forever; even the Spirit of truth; whom the world cannot receive, because it seeth Him not, neither knoweth Him: but ye know Him; for He dwelleth with you, and shall be in you. I will not leave you orphans: I will come to you." John 14:16-18, margin.

Before this the Spirit had been in the world; from the very beginning of the work of redemption He had been moving upon men's hearts. But while Christ was on earth, the disciples had desired no other helper. Not until they were deprived of His presence would they feel their need of the Spirit, and then He would come.

The Holy Spirit is Christ's representative, but divested of the personality of humanity, and independent thereof. Cumbered with humanity, Christ could not be in every place personally. Therefore it was for their interest that He should go to the Father, and send the Spirit to be His successor on earth. No one could then have any advantage because of his location or his personal contact with Christ. By the Spirit the Saviour would be accessible to all. In this sense He would be nearer to them than if He had not ascended on high.

"He that loveth Me shall be loved of My Father, and I will love him, and will manifest Myself to him." Jesus read the future of His disciples. He saw one brought to the scaffold, one to the cross, one to exile among the lonely rocks of the sea, others to persecution and death. He encouraged them with the promise that in every trial He would be with them. That promise has lost none of its force. The Lord knows all about His faithful servants who for His sake are lying in prison or who are banished to lonely islands. He comforts them with His own presence. When for the truth's sake the believer stands at the bar of unrighteous tribunals, Christ stands by his side. All the reproaches that fall upon him, fall upon Christ. Christ is condemned over again in the person of His disciple. When one is incarcerated in prison walls, Christ ravishes the heart with His love. When one suffers death for His sake, Christ says, "I am He that liveth, and was dead; and, behold, I am alive forevermore, . . . and have the keys of hell and of death." Rev. 1:18. The life that is sacrificed for Me is preserved unto eternal glory.

At all times and in all places, in all sorrows and in all afflictions, when the outlook seems dark and the future perplexing, and we feel helpless and alone, the Comforter will be sent in answer to the prayer of faith. Circumstances may separate us from every earthly friend; but no circumstance, no distance, can separate us from the heavenly Comforter. Wherever we are, wherever we may go, He is always at our right hand to support, sustain, uphold, and cheer.

The disciples still failed to understand Christ's words in their spiritual sense, and again He explained His meaning. By the Spirit, He said, He would manifest Himself to them. "The Comforter, which is the Holy Ghost, whom the Father will send in My name, He shall teach you all things." No more will you say, I cannot comprehend. No longer will you see through a glass, darkly. You shall "be able to comprehend with all saints what is the breadth, and length, and depth, and height; and to know the love of Christ, which passeth knowledge." Eph. 3:18, 19.

The disciples were to bear witness to the life and work of Christ. Through their word He was to speak to all the people on the face of the earth. But in the humiliation and death of Christ they were to suffer great trial and disappointment. That after this experience their word might be accurate, Jesus promised that the Comforter should "bring all things to your remembrance, whatsoever I have said unto you."

"I have yet many things to say unto you," He continued, "but ye cannot bear them now. Howbeit when He, the Spirit of truth, is come, He will guide you into all truth: for He shall not speak of Himself; but whatsoever He shall hear, that shall He speak: and He will show you things to come. He shall glorify Me: for He shall receive of Mine, and shall show it unto you." Jesus had opened before His disciples a vast tract of truth. But it was most difficult for them to keep His lessons distinct from the traditions and maxims of the scribes and Pharisees. They had been educated to accept the teaching of the rabbis as the voice of God, and it still held a power over their minds, and molded their sentiments. Earthly ideas, temporal things, still had a large place in their thoughts. They did not understand the spiritual nature of Christ's kingdom, though He had so often explained it to them.

Their minds had become confused. They did not comprehend the value of the Scriptures Christ presented. Many of His lessons seemed almost lost upon them. Jesus saw that they did not lay hold of the real meaning of His words. He compassionately promised that the Holy Spirit should recall these sayings to their minds. And He had left unsaid many things that could not be comprehended by the disciples. These also would be opened to them by the Spirit. The Spirit was to quicken their understanding, that they might have an appreciation of heavenly things. "When He, the Spirit of truth, is come," said Jesus, "He will guide you into all truth."

The Comforter is called "the Spirit of truth." His work is to define and maintain the truth. He first dwells in the heart as the Spirit of truth, and thus He becomes the Comforter. There is comfort and peace in the truth, but no real peace or comfort can be found in falsehood. It is through false theories and traditions that Satan gains his power over the mind. By directing men to false standards, he misshapes the character. Through the Scriptures the Holy Spirit speaks to the mind and impresses truth upon the heart. Thus He exposes error, and expels it from the soul. It is by the Spirit of truth, working through the word of God, that Christ subdues His chosen people to Himself.

In describing to His disciples the office work of the Holy Spirit, Jesus sought to inspire them with the joy and hope that inspired His own heart. He rejoiced because of the abundant help He had provided for His church. The Holy Spirit was the highest of all gifts that He could solicit from His Father for the exaltation of His people. The Spirit was to be given as a regenerating agent, and without this the sacrifice of Christ would have been of no avail. The power of evil had been strengthening for centuries, and the submission of men to this satanic captivity was amazing. Sin could be resisted and overcome only through the mighty agency of the Third Person of the Godhead, who would come with no modified energy, but in the fullness of divine power. It is the Spirit that makes effectual what has been wrought out by the world's Redeemer. It is by the Spirit that the heart is made pure. Through the Spirit the believer becomes a partaker of the divine nature. Christ has given His Spirit as a divine power to overcome all hereditary and cultivated tendencies to evil, and to impress His own character upon His church.

Of the Spirit Jesus said, "He shall glorify Me." The Saviour came to glorify the Father by the demonstration of His love; so the Spirit was to glorify Christ by revealing His grace to the world. The very image of God is to be reproduced in humanity. The honor of God, the honor of Christ, is involved in the perfection of the character of His people.

"When He [the Spirit of truth] is come, He will reprove the world of sin, and of righteousness, and of judgment." The preaching of the word will be of no avail without the continual presence and aid of the Holy Spirit. This is the only effectual teacher of divine truth. Only when the truth is accompanied to the heart by the Spirit will it quicken the conscience or transform the life. One might be able to present the letter of the word of God, he might be familiar with all its commands and promises; but unless the Holy Spirit sets home the truth, no souls will fall on the Rock and be broken. No amount of education, no advantage, however great, can make one a channel of light without the co-operation of the Spirit of God. The sowing of the gospel seed will not be a success unless the seed is quickened into life by the dew of heaven. Before one book of the New Testament was written, before one gospel sermon had been preached after Christ's ascension, the Holy Spirit came upon the praying apostles. Then the testimony of their enemies was, "Ye have filled Jerusalem with your doctrine." Acts 5:28.

Christ has promised the gift of the Holy Spirit to His church, and the promise belongs to us as much as to the first disciples. But like every other promise, it is given on conditions. There are many who believe and profess to claim the Lord's promise; they talk *about* Christ and *about* the Holy Spirit, yet receive no benefit. They do not surrender the soul to be guided and controlled by the divine agencies. We cannot use the Holy Spirit. The Spirit is to use us. Through the Spirit God works in His people "to will and to do of His good pleasure." Phil. 2:13. But many will not submit to this. They want to manage themselves. This is why they do not receive the heavenly gift. Only to those who wait humbly upon God, who watch for His guidance and grace, is the Spirit given. The power of God awaits their demand and reception. This promised blessing, claimed by faith, brings all other blessings in its train. It is given according to the riches of the grace of Christ, and He is ready to supply every soul according to the capacity to receive.

In His discourse to the disciples, Jesus made no mournful allusion to His own sufferings and death. His last legacy to them was a legacy of peace. He said, "Peace I leave with you, My peace I give unto you: not as the world giveth, give I unto you. Let not your heart be troubled, neither let it be afraid."

Before leaving the upper chamber, the Saviour led His disciples in a song of praise. His voice was heard, not in the strains of some mournful lament, but in the joyful notes of the Passover hallel:

"O praise the Lord, all ye nations:

Praise Him, all ye people.

For His merciful kindness is great toward us:

And the truth of the Lord endureth forever.

Praise ye the Lord." Psalm 117.

# Assignments: Lesson 8

## Principles of Pulpit Decorum

**Class assignment:**

Attend the tutorial "Principles of Pulpit Decorum" and read the related class notes.

**Reading assignment:**

E. G. White, *The Desire of Ages,* Chapter 26, "At Capernaum."

Luke 4:31-44.

**Written assignment:**

Note from your reading assignment the many skills that Jesus displayed when He spoke and ministered at the synagogue. Identify one which you would like to achieve and write a brief comment about it.

**Reading**

Ellen G. White, *The Desire of Ages* 252-261.

"At Capernaum"

At Capernaum Jesus dwelt in the intervals of His journeys to and fro, and it came to be known as "His own city." It was on the shores of the Sea of Galilee, and near the borders of the beautiful plain of Gennesaret, if not actually upon it.

The deep depression of the lake gives to the plain that skirts its shores the genial climate of the south. Here in the days of Christ flourished the palm tree and the olive, here were orchards and vineyards, green fields, and brightly blooming flowers in rich luxuriance, all watered by living streams bursting from the cliffs. The shores of the lake, and the hills that at a little distance encircle it, were dotted with towns and villages. The lake was covered with fishing boats. Everywhere was the stir of busy, active life.

Capernaum itself was well adapted to be the center of the Saviour's work. Being on the highway from Damascus to Jerusalem and Egypt, and to the Mediterranean Sea, it was a great thoroughfare of travel. People from many lands passed through the city, or tarried for rest in their journeyings to and fro. Here Jesus could meet all nations and all ranks, the rich and great as well as the poor and lowly, and His lessons would be carried to other countries and into many households. Investigation of the prophecies would thus be excited, attention would be directed to the Saviour, and His mission would be brought before the world.

Notwithstanding the action of the Sanhedrin against Jesus, the people eagerly awaited the development of His mission. All heaven was astir with interest. Angels were preparing the way for His ministry, moving upon men's hearts, and drawing them to the Saviour.

In Capernaum the nobleman's son whom Christ had healed was a witness to His power. And the court official and his household joyfully testified of their faith. When it was known that the Teacher Himself was among them, the whole city was aroused. Multitudes flocked to His presence. On the Sabbath the people crowded the synagogue until great numbers had to turn away, unable to find entrance.

All who heard the Saviour "were astonished at His doctrine: for His word was with power." "He taught them as one having authority, and not as the scribes." Luke 4:32; Matt. 7:29. The teaching of the scribes and elders was cold and formal, like a lesson learned by rote. To them the word of God possessed no vital power. Their own ideas and traditions were substituted for its teaching. In the accustomed round of service they professed to explain the law, but no inspiration from God stirred their own hearts or the hearts of their hearers.

Jesus had nothing to do with the various subjects of dissension among the Jews. It was His work to present the truth. His words shed a flood of light upon the teachings of patriarchs and prophets, and the Scriptures came to men as a new revelation. Never before had His hearers perceived such a depth of meaning in the word of God.

Jesus met the people on their own ground, as one who was acquainted with their perplexities. He made truth beautiful by presenting it in the most direct and simple way. His language was pure, refined, and clear as a running stream. His voice was as music to those who had listened to the monotonous tones of the rabbis. But while His teaching was simple, He spoke as one having authority. This characteristic set His teaching in contrast with that of all others. The rabbis spoke with doubt and hesitancy, as if the Scriptures might be interpreted to mean one thing or exactly the opposite. The hearers were daily involved in greater uncertainty. But Jesus taught the Scriptures as of unquestionable authority. Whatever His subject, it was presented with power, as if His words could not be controverted.

Yet He was earnest, rather than vehement. He spoke as one who had a definite purpose to fulfill. He was bringing to view the realities of the eternal world. In every theme God was revealed. Jesus sought to break the spell of infatuation which keeps men absorbed in earthly things. He placed the things of this life in their true relation, as subordinate to those of eternal interest; but He did not ignore their importance. He taught that heaven and earth are linked together, and that a knowledge of divine truth prepares men better to perform the duties of everyday life. He spoke as one familiar with heaven, conscious of His relationship to God, yet recognizing His unity with every member of the human family.

His messages of mercy were varied to suit His audience. He knew "how to speak a word in season to him that is weary" (Isa. 50:4); for grace was poured upon His lips, that He might convey to men in the most attractive way the treasures of truth. He had tact to meet the prejudiced minds, and surprise them with illustrations that won their attention. Through the imagination He reached the heart. His illustrations were taken from the things of daily life, and although they were simple, they had in them a wonderful depth of meaning. The birds of the air, the lilies of the field, the seed, the shepherd and the sheep,—with these objects Christ illustrated immortal truth; and ever afterward, when His hearers chanced to see these things of nature, they recalled His words. Christ's illustrations constantly repeated His lessons.

Christ never flattered men. He never spoke that which would exalt their fancies and imaginations, nor did He praise them for their clever inventions; but deep, unprejudiced thinkers received His teaching, and found that it tested their wisdom. They marveled at the spiritual truth expressed in the simplest language. The most highly educated were charmed with His words, and the uneducated were always profited. He had a message for the illiterate; and He made even the heathen to understand that He had a message for them.

His tender compassion fell with a touch of healing upon weary and troubled hearts. Even amid the turbulence of angry enemies He was surrounded with an atmosphere of peace. The beauty of His countenance, the loveliness of His character, above all, the love expressed in look and tone, drew to Him all who were not hardened in unbelief. Had it not been for the sweet, sympathetic spirit that shone out in every look and word, He would not have attracted the large congregations that He did. The afflicted ones who came to Him felt that He linked His interest with theirs as a faithful and tender friend, and they desired to know more of the truths He taught. Heaven was brought near. They longed to abide in His presence, that the comfort of His love might be with them continually.

Jesus watched with deep earnestness the changing countenances of His hearers. The faces that expressed interest and pleasure gave Him great satisfaction. As the arrows of truth pierced to the soul, breaking through the barriers of selfishness, and working contrition, and finally gratitude, the Saviour was made glad. When His eye swept over the throng of listeners, and He recognized among them the faces He had before seen, His countenance lighted up with joy. He saw in them hopeful subjects for His kingdom. When the truth, plainly spoken, touched some cherished idol, He marked the change of countenance, the cold, forbidding look, which told that the light was unwelcome. When He saw men refuse the message of peace, His heart was pierced to the very depths.

Jesus in the synagogue spoke of the kingdom He had come to establish, and of His mission to set free the captives of Satan. He was interrupted by a shriek of terror. A madman rushed forward from among the people, crying out, "Let us alone; what have we to do with Thee, Thou Jesus of Nazareth? art Thou come to destroy us? I know Thee who Thou art; the Holy One of God."

All was now confusion and alarm. The attention of the people was diverted from Christ, and His words were unheeded. This was Satan's purpose in leading his victim to the synagogue. But Jesus rebuked the demon, saying, "Hold thy peace, and come out of him. And when the devil had thrown him in the midst, he came out of him, and hurt him not."

The mind of this wretched sufferer had been darkened by Satan, but in the Saviour's presence a ray of light had pierced the gloom. He was roused to long for freedom from Satan's control; but the demon resisted the power of Christ. When the man tried to appeal to Jesus for help, the evil spirit put words into his mouth, and he cried out in an agony of fear. The demoniac partially comprehended that he was in the presence of One who could set him free; but when he tried to come within reach of that mighty hand, another's will held him, another's words found utterance through him. The conflict between the power of Satan and his own desire for freedom was terrible.

He who had conquered Satan in the wilderness of temptation was again brought face to face with His enemy. The demon exerted all his power to retain control of his victim. To lose ground here would be to give Jesus a victory. It seemed that the tortured man must lose his life in the struggle with the foe that had been the ruin of his manhood. But the Saviour spoke with authority, and set the captive free. The man who had been possessed stood before the wondering people happy in the freedom of self-possession. Even the demon had testified to the divine power of the Saviour.

The man praised God for his deliverance. The eye that had so lately glared with the fire of insanity, now beamed with intelligence, and overflowed with grateful tears. The people were dumb with amazement. As soon as they recovered speech they exclaimed, one to another, "What is this? a new teaching! with authority He commandeth even the unclean spirits, and they obey Him." Mark 1:27, R. V.

The secret cause of the affliction that had made this man a fearful spectacle to his friends and a burden to himself was in his own life. He had been fascinated by the pleasures of sin, and had thought to make life a grand carnival. He did not dream of becoming a terror to the world and the reproach of his family. He thought his time could be spent in innocent folly. But once in the downward path, his feet rapidly descended. Intemperance and frivolity perverted the noble attributes of his nature, and

Satan took absolute control of him.

Remorse came too late. When he would have sacrificed wealth and pleasure to regain his lost manhood, he had become helpless in the grasp of the evil one. He had placed himself on the enemy's ground, and Satan had taken possession of all his faculties. The tempter had allured him with many charming presentations; but when once the wretched man was in his power, the fiend became relentless in his cruelty, and terrible in his angry visitations. So it will be with all who yield to evil; the fascinating pleasure of their early career ends in the darkness of despair or the madness of a ruined soul.

The same evil spirit that tempted Christ in the wilderness, and that possessed the maniac of Capernaum, controlled the unbelieving Jews. But with them he assumed an air of piety, seeking to deceive them as to their motives in rejecting the Saviour. Their condition was more hopeless than that of the demoniac, for they felt no need of Christ and were therefore held fast under the power of Satan.

The period of Christ's personal ministry among men was the time of greatest activity for the forces of the kingdom of darkness. For ages Satan with his evil angels had been seeking to control the bodies and the souls of men, to bring upon them sin and suffering; then he had charged all this misery upon God. Jesus was revealing to men the character of God. He was breaking Satan's power, and setting his captives free. New life and love and power from heaven were moving upon the hearts of men, and the prince of evil was aroused to contend for the supremacy of his kingdom. Satan summoned all his forces, and at every step contested the work of Christ.

So it will be in the great final conflict of the controversy between righteousness and sin. While new life and light and power are descending from on high upon the disciples of Christ, a new life is springing up from beneath, and energizing the agencies of Satan. Intensity is taking possession of every earthly element. With a subtlety gained through centuries of conflict, the prince of evil works under a disguise. He appears clothed as an angel of light, and multitudes are "giving heed to seducing spirits, and doctrines of devils." 1 Tim. 4:1.

In the days of Christ the leaders and teachers of Israel were powerless to resist the work of Satan. They were neglecting the only means by which they could have withstood evil spirits. It was by the word of God that Christ overcame the wicked one. The leaders of Israel professed to be the expositors of God's word, but they had studied it only to sustain their traditions, and enforce their man-made observances. By their interpretation they made it express sentiments that God had never given. Their mystical construction made indistinct that which He had made plain. They disputed over insignificant technicalities, and practically denied the most essential truths.

Thus infidelity was sown broadcast. God's word was robbed of its power, and evil spirits worked their will.

History is repeating. With the open Bible before them, and professing to reverence its teachings, many of the religious leaders of our time are destroying faith in it as the word of God. They busy themselves with dissecting the word, and set their own opinions above its plainest statements. In their hands God's word loses its regenerating power. This is why infidelity runs riot, and iniquity is rife.

When Satan has undermined faith in the Bible, he directs men to other sources for light and power. Thus he insinuates himself. Those who turn from the plain teaching of Scripture and the convicting power of God's Holy Spirit are inviting the control of demons. Criticism and speculation concerning the Scriptures have opened the way for spiritism and theosophy—those modernized forms of ancient heathenism—to gain a foothold even in the professed churches of our Lord Jesus Christ.

Side by side with the preaching of the gospel, agencies are at work which are but the medium of lying spirits. Many a man tampers with these merely from curiosity, but seeing evidence of the working of a more than human power, he is lured on and on, until he is controlled by a will stronger than his own. He cannot escape from its mysterious power.

The defenses of the soul are broken down. He has no barrier against sin. When once the restraints of God's word and His Spirit are rejected, no man knows to what depths of degradation he may sink. Secret sin or master passion may hold him a captive as helpless as was the demoniac of Capernaum. Yet his condition is not hopeless.

The means by which we can overcome the wicked one is that by which Christ overcame,—the power of the word. God does not control our minds without our consent; but if we desire to know and to do His will, His promises are ours: "Ye shall know the truth, and the truth shall make you free." "If any man willeth to do His will, he shall know of the teaching." John 8:32; 7:17, R. V. Through faith in these promises, every man may be delivered from the snares of error and the control of sin.

Every man is free to choose what power he will have to rule over him. None have fallen so low, none are so vile, but that they can find deliverance in Christ. The demoniac, in place of prayer, could utter only the words of Satan; yet the heart's unspoken appeal was heard. No cry from a soul in need, though it fail of utterance in words, will be unheeded. Those who will consent to enter into covenant relation with the God of heaven are not left to the power of Satan or to the infirmity of their own nature. They are invited by the Saviour, "Let him take hold of My strength, that he may make peace with Me; and he shall make peace with Me." Isa. 27:5. The spirits of darkness will battle for the soul once under their dominion, but angels of God will contend for that soul with prevailing power. The Lord says, "Shall the prey be taken from the mighty, or the lawful captive delivered? . . . Thus saith the Lord, Even the captives of the mighty shall be taken away, and the prey of the terrible shall be delivered: for I will contend with him that contendeth with thee, and I will save thy children." Isa. 49:24, 25.

While the congregation in the synagogue were still spellbound with awe, Jesus withdrew to the home of Peter for a little rest. But here also a shadow had fallen. The mother of Peter's wife lay sick, stricken with a "great fever." Jesus rebuked the disease, and the sufferer arose, and ministered to the wants of the Master and His disciples.

Tidings of the work of Christ spread rapidly throughout Capernaum. For fear of the rabbis, the people dared not come for healing upon the Sabbath; but no sooner had the sun disappeared below the horizon than there was a great commotion. From the homes, the shops, the market places, the inhabitants of the city pressed toward the humble dwelling that sheltered Jesus. The sick were brought upon couches, they came leaning upon staffs, or, supported by friends, they tottered feebly into the Saviour's presence.

Hour after hour they came and went; for none could know whether tomorrow would find the Healer still among them. Never before had Capernaum witnessed a day like this. The air was filled with the voice of triumph and shouts of deliverance. The Saviour was joyful in the joy He had awakened. As He witnessed the sufferings of those who had come to Him, His heart was stirred with sympathy, and He rejoiced in His power to restore them to health and happiness.

Not until the last sufferer had been relieved did Jesus cease His work. It was far into the night when the multitude departed, and silence settled down upon the home of Simon. The long, exciting day was past, and Jesus sought rest. But while the city was still wrapped in slumber, the Saviour, "rising up a great while before day, . . . went out, and departed into a solitary place, and there prayed."

Thus were spent the days in the earthly life of Jesus. He often dismissed His disciples to visit their homes and rest; but He gently resisted their efforts to draw Him away from His labors. All day He toiled, teaching the ignorant, healing the sick, giving sight to the blind, feeding the multitude; and at the eventide or in the early morning, He went away to the sanctuary of the mountains for communion with His Father. Often He passed the entire night in prayer and meditation, returning at daybreak to His work among the people.

Early in the morning, Peter and his companions came to Jesus, saying that already the people of Capernaum were seeking Him. The disciples had been bitterly disappointed at the reception which Christ had met hitherto. The authorities at Jerusalem were seeking to murder Him; even His own townsmen had tried to take His life; but at Capernaum He was welcomed with joyful enthusiasm, and the hopes of the disciples kindled anew. It might be that among the liberty-loving Galileans were to be found the supporters of the new kingdom. But with surprise they heard Christ's words, "I must preach the kingdom of God to other cities also: for therefore am I sent."

In the excitement which then pervaded Capernaum, there was danger that the object of His mission would be lost sight of. Jesus was not satisfied to attract attention to Himself merely as a wonder worker or a healer of physical diseases. He was seeking to draw men to Him as their Saviour. While the people were eager to believe that He had come as a king, to establish an earthly reign, He desired to turn their minds away from the earthly to the spiritual. Mere worldly success would interfere with His work.

And the wonder of the careless crowd jarred upon His spirit. In His life no self-assertion mingled. The homage which the world gives to position, or wealth, or talent, was foreign to the Son of man. None of the means that men employ to win allegiance or command homage did Jesus use. Centuries before His birth, it had been prophesied of Him, "He shall not cry, nor lift up, nor cause His voice to be heard in the street. A bruised reed shall He not break, and the dimly burning flax shall He not quench: He shall bring forth judgment unto truth. He shall not fail nor be discouraged, till He have set judgment in the earth." Isa. 42:2-4, margin.

The Pharisees sought distinction by their scrupulous ceremonialism, and the ostentation of their worship and charities. They proved their zeal for religion by making it the theme of discussion. Disputes between opposing sects were loud and long, and it was not unusual to hear on the streets the voice of angry controversy from learned doctors of the law.

In marked contrast to all this was the life of Jesus. In that life no noisy disputation, no ostentatious worship, no act to gain applause, was ever witnessed. Christ was hid in God, and God was revealed in the character of His Son. To this revelation Jesus desired the minds of the people to be directed, and their homage to be given

The Sun of Righteousness did not burst upon the world in splendor, to dazzle the senses with His glory. It is written of Christ, "His going forth is prepared as the morning." Hosea 6:3. Quietly and gently the daylight breaks upon the earth, dispelling the shadow of darkness, and waking the world to life. So did the Sun of Righteousness arise, "with healing in His wings." Mal. 4:2.

# Assignments: Lesson 9

## Principles of Christian Communication

**Class assignment:**

Attend the tutorial "Principles of Christian Communication" and read the related class notes.

**Reading assignment:**

Matthew chapters 5-7.

**Written assignment:**

Compare the Five Principles of Christian Communication described in this lesson with Jesus' Sermon on the Mount (found in Matthew 5-7). Can you identify how Jesus met any of these five principles when He spoke to the crowd?

# Assignment: Lesson 10

## The Need, Nature, and Practice of Worship

**Class assignment:**

Attend the tutorial "The Need, Nature, and Practice of Worship" and read the related class notes.

**Reading assignment:**

E. G. White, *Testimonies to the Church,* Vol. 5:491-500.

E. G. White, *The Desire of Ages,* Chapter 17, "Nicodemus."

**Written assignment:**

What could a lay preacher do to help the pastor and elders enhance the worship hour? How do you think the lay preacher should approach the matter of making changes in the established pattern (or lack of pattern) in the church? How should the lay preacher go about planning hymns, prayers, and sermons for a congregation other than his or her own?

**Reading**

Ellen G. White, *Testimonies to the Church* 5:491-500.

"Behavior In The House Of God"

To the humble, believing soul, the house of God on earth is the gate of heaven. The song of praise, the prayer, the words spoken by Christ's representatives, are God's appointed agencies to prepare a people for the church above, for that loftier worship into which there can enter nothing that defileth.

From the sacredness which was attached to the earthly sanctuary, Christians may learn how they should regard the place where the Lord meets with His people. There has been a great change, not for the better, but for the worse, in the habits and customs of the people in reference to religious worship. The precious, the sacred, things which connect us with God are fast losing their hold upon our minds and hearts, and are being brought down to the level of common things. The reverence which the people had anciently for the sanctuary where they met with God in sacred service has largely passed away. Nevertheless, God Himself gave the order of His service, exalting it high above everything of a temporal nature.

The house is the sanctuary for the family, and the closet or the grove the most retired place for individual worship; but the church is the sanctuary for the congregation. There should be rules in regard to the time, the place, and the manner of worshiping. Nothing that is sacred, nothing that pertains to the worship of God, should be treated with carelessness or indifference. In order that men may do their best work in showing forth the praises of God, their associations must be such as will keep the sacred distinct from the common, in their minds. Those who have broad ideas, noble thoughts and aspirations, are those who have associations that strengthen all thoughts of divine things. Happy are those who have a sanctuary, be it high or low, in the city or among the rugged mountain caves, in the lowly cabin or in the wilderness. If it is the best they can secure for the Master, He will hallow the place with His presence, and it will be holy unto the Lord of hosts.

When the worshipers enter the place of meeting, they should do so with decorum, passing quietly to their seats. If there is a stove in the room, it is not proper to crowd about it in an indolent, careless attitude. Common talking, whispering, and laughing should not be permitted in the house of worship, either before or after the service. Ardent, active piety should characterize the worshipers.

If some have to wait a few minutes before the meeting begins, let them maintain a true spirit of devotion by silent meditation, keeping the heart uplifted to God in prayer that the service may be of special benefit to their own hearts and lead to the conviction and conversion of other souls. They should remember that heavenly messengers are in the house. We all lose much sweet communion with God by our restlessness, by not encouraging moments of reflection and prayer. The spiritual condition needs to be often reviewed and the mind and heart drawn toward the Sun of Righteousness. If when the people come into the house of worship, they have genuine reverence for the Lord and bear in mind that they are in His presence, there will be a sweet eloquence in silence. The whispering and laughing and talking which might be without sin in a common business place should find no sanction in the house where God is worshiped. The mind should be prepared to hear the word of God, that it may have due weight and suitably impress the heart.

When the minister enters, it should be with dignified, solemn mien. He should bow down in silent prayer as soon as he steps into the pulpit, and earnestly ask help of God. What an impression this will make! There will be solemnity and awe upon the people. Their minister is communing with God; he is committing himself to God before he dares to stand before the people. Solemnity rests upon all, and angels of God are brought very near. Every one of the congregation, also, who fears God should with bowed head unite in silent prayer with him that God may grace the meeting with His presence and give power to His truth proclaimed from human lips. When the meeting is opened by prayer, every knee should bow in the presence of the Holy One, and every heart should ascend to God in silent devotion. The prayers of faithful worshipers will be heard, and the ministry of the word will prove effectual. The lifeless attitude of the worshipers in the house of God is one great reason why the ministry is not more productive of good. The melody of song, poured forth from many hearts in clear, distinct utterance, is one of God's instrumentalities in the work of saving souls. All the service should be conducted with solemnity and awe, as if in the visible presence of the Master of assemblies.

When the word is spoken, you should remember, brethren, that you are listening to the voice of God through His delegated servant. Listen attentively. Sleep not for one instant, because by this slumber you may lose the very words that you need most—the very words which, if heeded, would save your feet from straying into wrong paths. Satan and his angels are busy creating a paralyzed condition of the senses so that cautions, warnings, and reproofs shall not be heard; or if heard, that they shall not take effect upon the heart and reform the life. Sometimes a little child may so attract the attention of the hearers that the precious seed does not fall into good ground and bring forth fruit. Sometimes young men and women have so little reverence for the house and worship of God that they keep up a continual communication with each other during the sermon. Could these see the angels of God looking upon them and marking their doings, they would be filled with shame, with abhorrence of themselves. God wants attentive hearers. It was while men slept that Satan sowed his tares.

When the benediction is pronounced, all should still be quiet, as if fearful of losing the peace of Christ. Let all pass out without jostling or loud talking, feeling that they are in the presence of God, that His eye is resting upon them, and that they must act as in His visible presence. Let there be no stopping in the aisles to visit or gossip, thus blocking them up so that others cannot pass out. The precincts of the church should be invested with a sacred reverence. It should not be made a place to meet old friends and visit and introduce common thoughts and worldly business transactions. These should be left outside the church. God and angels have been dishonored by the careless, noisy laughing and shuffling of feet heard in some places.

Parents, elevate the standard of Christianity in the minds of your children; help them to weave Jesus into their experience; teach them to have the highest reverence for the house of God and to understand that when they enter the Lord's house it should be with hearts that are softened and subdued by such thoughts as these: "God is here; this is His house. I must have pure thoughts and the holiest motives. I must have no pride, envy, jealousy, evil surmising, hatred, or deception in my heart, for I am coming into the presence of the holy God. This is the place where God meets with and blesses His people. The high and holy One who inhabiteth eternity looks upon me, searches my heart, and reads the most secret thoughts and acts of my life."

Brethren, will you not devote a little thought to this subject and notice how you conduct yourselves in the house of God and what efforts you are making by precept and example to cultivate reverence in your children? You roll vast responsibilities upon the preacher and hold him accountable for the souls of your children; but you do not sense your own responsibility as parents and as instructors and, like Abraham, command your household after you, that they may keep the statutes of the Lord. Your sons and daughters are corrupted by your own example and lax precepts; and, notwithstanding this lack of domestic training, you expect the minister to counteract your daily work and accomplish the wonderful achievement of training their hearts and lives to virtue and piety. After the minister has done all he can do for the church by faithful, affectionate admonition, patient discipline, and fervent prayer to reclaim and save the soul, yet is not successful, the fathers and mothers often blame him because their children are not converted, when it may be because of their own neglect. The burden rests with the parents; and will they take up the work that God has entrusted to them, and with fidelity perform it? Will they move onward and upward, working in a humble, patient, persevering way to reach the exalted standard themselves and to bring their children up with them? No wonder our churches are feeble and do not have that deep, earnest piety in their borders that they should have. Our present habits and customs, which dishonor God and bring the sacred and heavenly down to the level of the common, are against us. We have a sacred, testing, sanctifying truth; and if our habits and practices are not in accordance with the truth, we are sinners against great light, and are proportionately guilty. It will be far more tolerable for the heathen in the day of God's retributive justice than for us.

A much greater work might be done than we are now doing in reflecting the light of truth. God expects us to bear much fruit. He expects greater zeal and faithfulness, more affectionate and earnest efforts, by the individual members of the church for their neighbors and for those who are out of Christ. Parents must begin their work on a high plane of action. All who name the name of Christ must put on the whole armor and entreat, warn, and seek to win souls from sin. Lead all you can to listen to the truth in the house of God. We must do much more than we are doing to snatch souls from the burning.

It is too true that reverence for the house of God has become almost extinct. Sacred things and places are not discerned; the holy and exalted are not appreciated. Is there not a cause for the want of fervent piety in our families? Is it not because the high standard of religion is left to trail in the dust? God gave rules of order, perfect and exact, to His ancient people. Has His character changed? Is He not the great and mighty God who rules in the heaven of heavens? Would it not be well for us often to read the directions given by God Himself to the Hebrews, that we who have the light of the glorious truth shining upon us may imitate their reverence for the house of God? We have abundant reason to maintain a fervent, devoted spirit in the worship of God. We have reason even to be more thoughtful and reverential in our worship than had the Jews. But an enemy has been at work to destroy our faith in the sacredness of Christian worship.

The place dedicated to God should not be a room where worldly business is transacted. If the children assemble to worship God in a room that is used during the week for a school or a storeroom, they will be more than human if, mingled with their devotional thoughts, they do not also have thoughts of their studies or of things that have happened during the week. The education and training of the youth should be of a character that would exalt sacred things and encourage pure devotion for God in His house. Many who profess to be children of the heavenly King have no true appreciation of the sacredness of eternal things. Nearly all need to be taught how to conduct themselves in the house of God. Parents should not only teach, but command, their children to enter the sanctuary with sobriety and reverence.

The moral taste of the worshipers in God's holy sanctuary must be elevated, refined, sanctified. This matter has been sadly neglected. Its importance has been overlooked, and as the result, disorder and irreverence have become prevalent, and God has been dishonored. When the leaders in the church, ministers and people, father and mothers, have not had elevated views of this matter, what could be expected of the inexperienced children? They are too often found in groups, away from the parents, who should have charge of them. Notwithstanding they are in the presence of God, and His eye is looking upon them, they are light and trifling, they whisper and laugh, are careless, irreverent, and inattentive. They are seldom instructed that the minister is God's ambassador, that the message he brings is one of God's appointed agencies in the salvation of souls, and that to all who have the privilege brought within their reach it will be a savor of life unto life or of death unto death.

The delicate and susceptible minds of the youth obtain their estimate of the labors of God's servants by the way their parents treat the matter. Many heads of families make the service a subject of criticism at home, approving a few things and condemning others. Thus the message of God to men is criticized and questioned, and made a subject of levity. What impressions are thus made upon the young by these careless, irreverent remarks the books of heaven alone will reveal. The children see and understand these things very much quicker than parents are apt to think. Their moral senses receive a wrong bias that time will never fully change. The parents mourn over the hardness of heart in their children and the difficulty in arousing their moral sensibility to answer to the claims of God. But the books of heavenly record trace with unerring pen the true cause. The parents were unconverted. They were not in harmony with heaven or with heaven's work. Their low, common ideas of the sacredness of the ministry and of the sanctuary of God were woven into the education of their children. It is a question whether anyone who has for years been under this blighting influence of home instruction will ever have a sensitive reverence and high regard for God's ministry and the agencies He has appointed for the salvation of souls. These things should be spoken of with reverence, with propriety of language, and with fine susceptibility, that you may reveal to all you associate with that you regard the message from God's servants as a message to you from God Himself.

Parents, be careful what example and what ideas you give your children. Their minds are plastic, and impressions are easily made. In regard to the service of the sanctuary, if the speaker has a blemish, be afraid to mention it. Talk only of the good work he is doing, of the good ideas he presented, which you should heed as coming through God's agent. It may be readily seen why children are so little impressed with the ministry of the word and why they have so little reverence for the house of God. Their education has been defective in this respect. Their parents need daily communion with God. Their own ideas need to be refined and ennobled; their lips need to be touched with a live coal from off the altar; then their habits, their practices at home, will make a good impression on the minds and characters of their children. The standard of religion will be greatly elevated. Such parents will do a great work for God. They will have less earthliness, less sensuality, and more refinement and fidelity at home. Life will be invested with a solemnity of which they have scarcely conceived. Nothing will be made common that pertains to the service and worship of God.

I am often pained as I enter the house where God is worshiped, to see the untidy dress of both men and women. If the heart and character were indicated by the outward apparel, then certainly nothing could be heavenly about them. They have no true idea of the order, the neatness, and the refined deportment that God requires of all who come into His presence to worship Him. What impressions do these things give to unbelievers and to the youth, who are keen to discern and to draw their conclusions?

In the minds of many there are no more sacred thoughts connected with the house of God than with the most common place. Some will enter the place of worship with their hats on, in soiled, dirty clothes. Such do not realize that they are to meet with God and holy angels. There should be a radical change in this matter all through our churches. Ministers themselves need to elevate their ideas, to have finer susceptibilities in regard to it. It is a feature of the work that has been sadly neglected. Because of the irreverence in attitude, dress, and deportment, and lack of a worshipful frame of mind, God has often turned His face away from those assembled for His worship.

All should be taught to be neat, clean, and orderly in their dress, but not to indulge in that external adorning which is wholly inappropriate for the sanctuary. There should be no display of the apparel; for this encourages irreverence. The attention of the people is often called to this or that fine article of dress, and thus thoughts are intruded that should have no place in the hearts of the worshipers. God is to be the subject of thought, the object of worship; and anything that attracts the mind from the solemn, sacred service is an offense to Him. The parading of bows and ribbons, ruffles and feathers, and gold and silver ornaments is a species of idolatry and is wholly inappropriate for the sacred service of God, where the eye of every worshiper should be single to His glory. All matters of dress should be strictly guarded, following closely the Bible rule. Fashion has been the goddess who has ruled the outside world, and she often insinuates herself into the church. The church should make the word of God her standard, and parents should think intelligently upon this subject. When they see their children inclined to follow worldly fashions, they should, like Abraham, resolutely command their households after them. Instead of uniting them with the world, connect them with God. Let none dishonor God's sanctuary by their showy apparel. God and angels are there. The Holy One of Israel has spoken through His apostle: "Whose adorning let it not be that outward adorning of plaiting the hair, and of wearing of gold, or of putting on of apparel; but let it be the hidden man of the heart, in that which is not corruptible, even the ornament of a meek and quiet spirit, which is in the sight of God of great price."

When a church has been raised up and left uninstructed on these points, the minister has neglected his duty and will have to give an account to God for the impressions he allowed to prevail. Unless correct ideas of true worship and true reverence are impressed upon the people, there will be a growing tendency to place the sacred and eternal on a level with common things, and those professing the truth will be an offense to God and a disgrace to religion. They can never, with their uncultivated ideas, appreciate a pure and holy heaven, and be prepared to join with the worshipers in the heavenly courts above, where all is purity and perfection, where every being has perfect reverence for God and His holiness.

Paul describes the work of God's ambassadors as that by which every man shall be presented perfect in Christ Jesus. Those who embrace the truth of heavenly origin should be refined, ennobled, sanctified through it. It will require much painstaking effort to reach God's standard of true manhood. The irregular stones hewed from the quarry must be chiseled, their rough sides must be polished. This is an age famous for surface work, for easy methods, for boasted holiness aside from the standard of character that

God has erected. All short routes, all cutoff tracks, all teaching which fails to exalt the law of God as the standard of religious character, is spurious. Perfection of character is a lifelong work, unattainable by those who are not willing to strive for it in God's appointed way, by slow and toilsome steps. We cannot afford to make any mistake in this matter, but we want day by day to be growing up into Christ, our living Head.

Ellen G. White, *The Desire of Ages* 167-177.

"Nicodemus"

Nicodemus held a high position of trust in the Jewish nation. He was highly educated, and possessed talents of no ordinary character, and he was an honored member of the national council. With others, he had been stirred by the teaching of Jesus. Though rich, learned, and honored, he had been strangely attracted by the humble Nazarene. The lessons that had fallen from the Saviour's lips had greatly impressed him, and he desired to learn more of these wonderful truths.

Christ's exercise of authority in the cleansing of the temple had roused the determined hatred of the priests and rulers. They feared the power of this stranger. Such boldness on the part of an obscure Galilean was not to be tolerated. They were bent on putting an end to His work. But not all were agreed in this purpose. There were some that feared to oppose One who was so evidently moved upon by the Spirit of God. They remembered how prophets had been slain for rebuking the sins of the leaders in Israel. They knew that the bondage of the Jews to a heathen nation was the result of their stubbornness in rejecting reproofs from God. They feared that in plotting against Jesus the priests and rulers were following in the steps of their fathers, and would bring fresh calamities upon the nation. Nicodemus shared these feelings. In a council of the Sanhedrin, when the course to be pursued toward Jesus was considered, Nicodemus advised caution and moderation. He urged that if Jesus was really invested with authority from God, it would be perilous to reject His warnings. The priests dared not disregard this counsel, and for the time they took no open measures against the Saviour.

Since hearing Jesus, Nicodemus had anxiously studied the prophecies relating to the Messiah; and the more he searched, the stronger was his conviction that this was the One who was to come. With many others in Israel he had been greatly distressed by the profanation of the temple. He was a witness of the scene when Jesus drove out the buyers and the sellers; he beheld the wonderful manifestation of divine power; he saw the Saviour receiving the poor and healing the sick; he saw their looks of joy, and heard their words of praise; and he could not doubt that Jesus of Nazareth was the Sent of God.

He greatly desired an interview with Jesus, but shrank from seeking Him openly. It would be too humiliating for a ruler of the Jews to acknowledge himself in sympathy with a teacher as yet so little known. And should his visit come to the knowledge of the Sanhedrin, it would draw upon him their scorn and denunciation. He resolved upon a secret interview, excusing this on the ground that if he were to go openly, others might follow his example. Learning by special inquiry the Saviour's place of retirement in the Mount of Olives, he waited until the city was hushed in slumber, and then sought Him.

In the presence of Christ, Nicodemus felt a strange timidity, which he endeavored to conceal under an air of composure and dignity. "Rabbi," he said, "we know that Thou art a teacher come from God: for no man can do these miracles that Thou doest, except God be with him." By speaking of Christ's rare gifts as a teacher, and also of His wonderful power to perform miracles, he hoped to pave the way for his interview. His words were designed to express and to invite confidence; but they really expressed unbelief. He did not acknowledge Jesus to be the Messiah, but only a teacher sent from God.

Instead of recognizing this salutation, Jesus bent His eyes upon the speaker, as if reading his very soul. In His infinite wisdom He saw before Him a seeker after truth. He knew the object of this visit, and with a desire to deepen the conviction already resting upon His listener's mind, He came directly to the point, saying solemnly, yet kindly, "Verily, verily, I say unto thee, Except a man be born from above, he cannot see the kingdom of God." John 3:3, margin.

Nicodemus had come to the Lord thinking to enter into a discussion with Him, but Jesus laid bare the foundation principles of truth. He said to Nicodemus, It is not theoretical knowledge you need so much as spiritual regeneration. You need not to have your curiosity satisfied, but to have a new heart. You must receive a new life from above before you can appreciate heavenly things. Until this change takes place, making all things new, it will result in no saving good for you to discuss with Me My authority or My mission.

Nicodemus had heard the preaching of John the Baptist concerning repentance and baptism, and pointing the people to One who should baptize with the Holy Spirit. He himself had felt that there was a lack of spirituality among the Jews, that, to a great degree, they were controlled by bigotry and worldly ambition. He had hoped for a better state of things at the Messiah's coming. Yet the heart-searching message of the Baptist had failed to work in him conviction of sin. He was a strict Pharisee, and prided himself on his good works. He was widely esteemed for his benevolence and his liberality in sustaining the temple service, and he felt secure of the favor of God. He was startled at the thought of a kingdom too pure for him to see in his present state.

The figure of the new birth, which Jesus had used, was not wholly unfamiliar to Nicodemus. Converts from heathenism to the faith of Israel were often compared to children just born. Therefore he must have perceived that the words of Christ were not to be taken in a literal sense. But by virtue of his birth as an Israelite he regarded himself as sure of a place in the kingdom of God. He felt that he needed no change. Hence his surprise at the Saviour's words. He was irritated by their close application to himself. The pride of the Pharisee was struggling against the honest desire of the seeker after truth. He wondered that Christ should speak to him as He did, not respecting his position as ruler in Israel.

Surprised out of his self-possession, he answered Christ in words full of irony, "How can a man be born when he is old?" Like many others when cutting truth is brought home to the conscience, he revealed the fact that the natural man receiveth not the things of the Spirit of God. There is in him nothing that responds to spiritual things; for spiritual things are spiritually discerned.

But the Saviour did not meet argument with argument. Raising His hand with solemn, quiet dignity, He pressed the truth home with greater assurance, "Verily, verily, I say unto thee, Except a man be born of water and of the Spirit, he cannot enter into the kingdom of God." Nicodemus knew that Christ here referred to water baptism and the renewing of the heart by the Spirit of God. He was convinced that he was in the presence of the One whom John the Baptist had foretold.

Jesus continued: "That which is born of the flesh is flesh; and that which is born of the Spirit is spirit." By nature the heart is evil, and "who can bring a clean thing out of an unclean? not one." Job 14:4. No human invention can find a remedy for the sinning soul. "The carnal mind is enmity against God: for it is not subject to the law of God, neither indeed can be." "Out of the heart proceed evil thoughts, murders, adulteries, fornications, thefts, false witness, blasphemies." Rom. 8:7; Matt. 15:19. The fountain of the heart must be purified before the streams can become pure. He who is trying to reach heaven by his own works in keeping the law is attempting an impossibility. There is no safety for one who has merely a legal religion, a form of godliness. The Christian's life is not a modification or improvement of the old, but a transformation of nature. There is a death to self and sin, and a new life altogether. This change can be brought about only by the effectual working of the Holy Spirit.

Nicodemus was still perplexed, and Jesus used the wind to illustrate His meaning: "The wind bloweth where it listeth, and thou hearest the sound thereof, but canst not tell whence it cometh, and whither it goeth: so is everyone that is born of the Spirit."

The wind is heard among the branches of the trees, rustling the leaves and flowers; yet it is invisible, and no man knows whence it comes or whither it goes. So with the work of the Holy Spirit upon the heart. It can no more be explained than can the movements of the wind. A person may not be able to tell the exact time or place, or to trace all the circumstances in the process of conversion; but this does not prove him to be unconverted. By an agency as unseen as the wind, Christ is constantly working upon the heart. Little by little, perhaps unconsciously to the receiver, impressions are made that tend to draw the soul to Christ. These may be received through meditating upon Him, through reading the Scriptures, or through hearing the word from the living preacher. Suddenly, as the Spirit comes with more direct appeal, the soul gladly surrenders itself to Jesus. By many this is called sudden conversion; but it is the result of long wooing by the Spirit of God,—a patient, protracted process.

While the wind is itself invisible, it produces effects that are seen and felt. So the work of the Spirit upon the soul will reveal itself in every act of him who has felt its saving power. When the Spirit of God takes possession of the heart, it transforms the life. Sinful thoughts are put away, evil deeds are renounced; love, humility, and peace take the place of anger, envy, and strife. Joy takes the place of sadness, and the countenance reflects the light of heaven. No one sees the hand that lifts the burden, or beholds the light descend from the courts above. The blessing comes when by faith the soul surrenders itself to God. Then that power which no human eye can see creates a new being in the image of God.

It is impossible for finite minds to comprehend the work of redemption. Its mystery exceeds human knowledge; yet he who passes from death to life realizes that it is a divine reality. The beginning of redemption we may know here through a personal experience. Its results reach through the eternal ages.

While Jesus was speaking, some gleams of truth penetrated the ruler's mind. The softening, subduing influence of the Holy Spirit impressed his heart. Yet he did not fully understand the Saviour's words. He was not so much impressed by the necessity of the new birth as by the manner of its accomplishment. He said wonderingly, "How can these things be?"

"Art thou a master of Israel, and knowest not these things?" Jesus asked. Surely one entrusted with the religious instruction of the people should not be ignorant of truths so important. His words conveyed the lesson that instead of feeling irritated over the plain words of truth, Nicodemus should have had a very humble opinion of himself, because of his spiritual ignorance. Yet Christ spoke with such solemn dignity, and both look and tone expressed such earnest love, that Nicodemus was not offended as he realized his humiliating condition.

But as Jesus explained that His mission on earth was to establish a spiritual instead of a temporal kingdom, His hearer was troubled. Seeing this, Jesus added, "If I have told you earthly things, and ye believe not, how shall ye believe, if I tell you of heavenly things?" If Nicodemus could not receive Christ's teaching, illustrating the work of grace upon the heart, how could he comprehend the nature of His glorious heavenly kingdom? Not discerning the nature of Christ's work on earth, he could not understand His work in heaven.

The Jews whom Jesus had driven from the temple claimed to be children of Abraham, but they fled from the Saviour's presence because they could not endure the glory of God which was manifested in Him. Thus they gave evidence that they were not fitted by the grace of God to participate in the sacred services of the temple. They were zealous to maintain an appearance of holiness, but they neglected holiness of heart. While they were sticklers for the letter of the law, they were constantly violating its spirit. Their great need was that very change which Christ had been explaining to Nicodemus,—a new moral birth, a cleansing from sin, and a renewing of knowledge and holiness.

There was no excuse for the blindness of Israel in regard to the work of regeneration. Under the inspiration of the Holy Spirit, Isaiah had written, "We are all as an unclean thing, and all our righteousnesses are as filthy rags." David had prayed, "Create in me a clean heart, O God; and renew a right spirit within me." And through Ezekiel the promise had been given, "A new heart also will I give you, and a new spirit will I put within you: and I will take away the stony heart out of your flesh, and I will give you an heart of flesh. And I will put My Spirit within you, and cause you to walk in My statutes." Isa. 64:6; Ps. 51:10; Ezek. 36:26, 27.

Nicodemus had read these scriptures with a clouded mind; but he now began to comprehend their meaning. He saw that the most rigid obedience to the mere letter of the law as applied to the outward life could entitle no man to enter the kingdom of heaven. In the estimation of men, his life had been just and honorable; but in the presence of Christ he felt that his heart was unclean, and his life unholy.

Nicodemus was being drawn to Christ. As the Saviour explained to him concerning the new birth, he longed to have this change wrought in himself. By what means could it be accomplished? Jesus answered the unspoken question: "As Moses lifted up the serpent in the wilderness, even so must the Son of man be lifted up: that whosoever believeth in Him should not perish, but have eternal life."

Here was ground with which Nicodemus was familiar. The symbol of the uplifted serpent made plain to him the Saviour's mission. When the people of Israel were dying from the sting of the fiery serpents, God directed Moses to make a serpent of brass, and place it on high in the midst of the congregation. Then the word was sounded throughout the encampment that all who would look upon the serpent should live. The people well knew that in itself the serpent had no power to help them. It was a symbol of Christ. As the image made in the likeness of the destroying serpents was lifted up for their healing, so One made "in the likeness of sinful flesh" was to be their Redeemer. Rom. 8:3. Many of the Israelites regarded the sacrificial service as having in itself virtue to set them free from sin. God desired to teach them that it had no more value than that serpent of brass. It was to lead their minds to the Saviour. Whether for the healing of their wounds or the pardon of their sins, they could do nothing for themselves but show their faith in the Gift of God. They were to look and live.

Those who had been bitten by the serpents might have delayed to look. They might have questioned how there could be efficacy in that brazen symbol. They might have demanded a scientific explanation. But no explanation was given. They must accept the word of God to them through Moses. To refuse to look was to perish.

Not through controversy and discussion is the soul enlightened. We must look and live. Nicodemus received the lesson, and carried it with him. He searched the Scriptures in a new way, not for the discussion of a theory, but in order to receive life for the soul. He began to see the kingdom of heaven as he submitted himself to the leading of the Holy Spirit.

There are thousands today who need to learn the same truth that was taught to Nicodemus by the uplifted serpent. They depend on their obedience to the law of God to commend them to His favor. When they are bidden to look to Jesus, and believe that He saves them solely through His grace, they exclaim, "How can these things be?"

Like Nicodemus, we must be willing to enter into life in the same way as the chief of sinners. Than Christ, "there is none other name under heaven given among men, whereby we must be saved." Acts 4:12. Through faith we receive the grace of God; but faith is not our Saviour. It earns nothing. It is the hand by which we lay hold upon Christ, and appropriate His merits, the remedy for sin. And we cannot even repent without the aid of the Spirit of God. The Scripture says of Christ, "Him hath God exalted with His right hand to be a Prince and a Saviour, for to give repentance to Israel, and forgiveness of sins." Acts 5:31. Repentance comes from Christ as truly as does pardon.

How, then, are we to be saved? "As Moses lifted up the serpent in the wilderness," so the Son of man has been lifted up, and everyone who has been deceived and bitten by the serpent may look and live. "Behold the Lamb of God, which taketh away the sin of the world." John 1:29. The light shining from the cross reveals the love of God. His love is drawing us to Himself. If we do not resist this drawing, we shall be led to the foot of the cross in repentance for the sins that have crucified the Saviour. Then the Spirit of God through faith produces a new life in the soul. The thoughts and desires are brought into obedience to the will of Christ. The heart, the mind, are created anew in the image of Him who works in us to subdue all things to Himself. Then the law of God is written in the mind and heart, and we can say with Christ, "I delight to do Thy will, O my God." Ps. 40:8.

In the interview with Nicodemus, Jesus unfolded the plan of salvation, and His mission to the world. In none of His subsequent discourses did He explain so fully, step by step, the work necessary to be done in the hearts of all who would inherit the kingdom of heaven. At the very beginning of His ministry He opened the truth to a member of the Sanhedrin, to the mind that was most receptive, and to an appointed teacher of the people. But the leaders of Israel did not welcome the light. Nicodemus hid the truth in his heart, and for three years there was little apparent fruit.

But Jesus was acquainted with the soil into which He cast the seed. The words spoken at night to one listener in the lonely mountain were not lost. For a time Nicodemus did not publicly acknowledge Christ, but he watched His life, and pondered His teachings. In the Sanhedrin council he repeatedly thwarted the schemes of the priests to destroy Him. When at last Jesus was lifted up on the cross, Nicodemus remembered the teaching upon Olivet: "As Moses lifted up the serpent in the wilderness, even so must the Son of man be lifted up: that whosoever believeth in Him should not perish, but have eternal life." The light from that secret interview illumined the cross upon Calvary, and Nicodemus saw in Jesus the world's Redeemer.

After the Lord's ascension, when the disciples were scattered by persecution, Nicodemus came boldly to the front. He employed his wealth in sustaining the infant church that the Jews had expected to be blotted out at the death of Christ. In the time of peril he who had been so cautious and questioning was firm as a rock, encouraging the faith of the disciples, and furnishing means to carry forward the work of the gospel. He was scorned and persecuted by those who had paid him reverence in other days. He became poor in this world's goods; yet he faltered not in the faith which had its beginning in that night conference with Jesus.

Nicodemus related to John the story of that interview, and by his pen it was recorded for the instruction of millions. The truths there taught are as important today as they were on that solemn night in the shadowy mountain, when the Jewish ruler came to learn the way of life from the lowly Teacher of Galilee.

# Assignment: Lesson 11

## Introduction to African-American Preaching

**Class assignment:**

Attend the tutorial "Introduction to African-American Preaching" and read the related class notes.

**Written assignment:**

Prepare your exam sermon, limited strictly to 10 minutes minimum and 12 minutes maximum. This is to be preached to the class at the next meeting and assessed by your peer group as well as the class tutor. It can also be videotaped for personal assessment.